Discipleship Books:

The Ministry of Jesus

By

Philip Watson

Dedication

Dedicated to my loving wife Dianne, and my three children, Andrew, Jonathon and Ruth.

My grateful thanks for allowing me to spend so much of my spare time writing these words.

Acknowledgements

My grateful thanks to Warren Portsmouth who patiently helped me review the manuscripts of this book and other books. Warren suggested improvements and asked questions at appropriate points. He was also instrumental in the design of the covers of this book and others in the series.

I also want to acknowledge the help of the Holy Spirit for inspiring me to write these books and for frequently reminding me of scriptures, relevant to topics, in each book.

This book is part of a quintet of books about Jesus. The other titles being:

The Son

The Incarnation of Jesus

Jesus changed our lives.

Other books written by Philip Watson:

Great relationships

The Holy Spirit

Great Summaries

100 Spiritual Principles

Books Coming Soon

    1200 Great Quotes

    Attitude In the Old Testament

    Evidence The Bible Is True

    Creation or Evolution

    The Father

Contents

Introduction

The content of this book could be summarised as:

What Jesus did during his ministry.

Why he did it, and the

Way he did it

and that content is detailed for one purpose that we can follow closely in his footsteps in our ministry - whatever that may be.

Before arriving at what Jesus did during his ministry, a quick reviewed of what Jesus said;

about the purposes of his ministry, offers ample thought about ways we can follow in his footsteps - and why.

Jesus certainly knew what he was doing! At the beginning of his ministry he defined his mission statement.

> The Spirit of the Lord is on me,
> because he has anointed me
> to preach good news to the poor.
> He has sent me to proclaim
> freedom for the prisoners
> and recovery of sight for the blind,
> to release the oppressed,
> to proclaim the year of the Lord's favor.
> Luke 4:18-19

At other times, Jesus spoke about the purposes for which he had come to this Earth.

- For even the Son of Man did not come to be served; he came to serve and to give his life to redeem many people. Mark 10.45 (G.N)

- For the Son of Man came to seek and to save what was lost. Luke 19.10

- For I have not come to call the righteous, but sinners. Matt 9.13

- The thief comes to steal and kill and destroy; I have come that they might have life and have it to the full. John

10.10

Jesus not only defined his own mission statement and goals, but made it clear to his disciples who he was - reminding them that he was not merely, a carpenter from Nazareth.   He said;

- "I am the bread of life." John 6:35

- "I am the good shepherd." John 10:11

- "I am the gate for the sheep." John 10:7

- "I am the light of the world." John 8:12

- "I am the resurrection and the life." John 11:25

- "I am the vine and my father is the gardener." John 15:1

- "I am the way, and the truth, and the life; no one comes to the Father but by me." John 14:6

Note, Jesus began each statement with the words, "I am", they are the same words God used when he spoke to Moses.

Another feature of Jesus ministry was that he aimed to achieve his ministry goals, in a definite time-frame.   During his ministry he asked his disciples, "How long will I be with you" and then near the end of his ministry, told them explicitly. "Now I am going.." John 16:5 NIV

Then there were his plans and goals for his disciples.

(a) He 'called' his disciples to follow him rather than follow the practice, of the time, which was to gradually gather disciples.

(b) He wanted a band of disciples who would be leaders of the future Church. Even while   he was calling them to follow him; he indicated the purpose of their calling, was to be, fishers of men and women.

(c) He knew they needed to be trained for their   role as fishers of men and women, so he sent them out on, trial, ministry trips. To learn the trade, so to speak. E.g. Matt 10.

(d) Jesus gave them, private staff training sessions, to prepare them for when he was gone. E.g. John 14-16

(e) He created a vision in their minds of a great harvest, that was waiting   to be reaped. Luke 10:2

(f) He taught them that to be successful harvesters,   they would have to be 100% committed to the kingdom of God (Matt 6:33) and fully use their talents. Matt 25:14-30

(g) Jesus also had marker points along the way, to measure the disciples progress in   understanding. Before he left this Earth, he wanted to be sure they understood who he was, so he asked them, "Who do you say I am?" Matt 16:15

(h) The first time Jesus met the twelve, he indicated the purpose of calling them. They were to become fishers of men and women. Among his final words to them was a world wide commission, to make disciples of all nations.

(i) The disciples knew they had been given training and   clearly defined goals,   but Jesus knew they would need more than clearly defined goals to achieve the purposes he had given them. The disciples would   need   a glue, to bind them together. That glue, was love and he commanded them to love one another. John 15:12 I.e. Love was not an optional extra for the disciples. It was   a command.

(j) The power to achieve the great commission he had given them, was to come from the same Holy Spirit who had helped Jesus begin, and complete his ministry. Power from the Holy Spirit. So he told them "wait" till he comes.

Just from what Jesus said, there is plenty to chew over when pondering, our ministry as Christians.

What Jesus said.

Chapter 1

His words – our definition.

What can we take from   what has been written so far? A graduate from a business school is likely to   be impressed with Jesus because, two thousand years before there were Business Schools, Jesus was employing business models.

  He had a mission statement. He clearly defined goals (the "I have come...statements). He defined who he was (the "I am...statements) and he had a time-frame within which, to achieve his goals. And the same clarity, was evident in plans and goals, for   his disciples.

But, from there, his pathway and the pathway for most   graduates of a business schools, is likely to   diverge. For example, Jesus said he had come to establish a kingdom that would 'not' have a head-office on Earth. I.e. "my kingdom is not of this world." John 18:36 NLT

And   soon   after   he   established   the organisation (which we call   the Church) whose purpose was to make new disciples, the CEO (Jesus),   said he was going to, disappear into heaven. Now that is not an earthly plan!

While   there   are   both   similarities   and differences to business models, the purpose of this chapter is not to get too involved in either the similarities or the differences. The purpose is to focus on the clarity Jesus had for his ministry. And that clarity, makes it easy for us to identify ways to follow in his footsteps - with our ministry.

By using the word 'ministry', some readers may be, beginning to think. 'This book is probably not for me because I do not work full-time or part-time in a Church or Christian organisation, so I am not in ministry!

That is not how Jesus thought. In his thinking,

everyone is called to be a disciple who will follow in his footsteps; and Jesus came to serve.

Near the top of the weekly newsletter of a Church we sometimes attend, while on holiday, are these words.

Pastor. (name of the pastor). Minister: everyone in the congregation.

That simple slogan is a reminder that whatever denomination or Church we worship in, there will be a leader or leaders variously called; Priest/s or Minister/s or Pastor/s, but that everyone in the congregation is meant to be a minister, in some way.

The Apostle Paul called himself and his co-workers Timothy and Titus, "ministers of a new covenant", and the author of the book of Hebrews called angels, "ministering spirits". Heb 1:14 & 2 Cor 3:6

The English word *minister* is a translation of the Hebrew word *Sarat,* which means: "to serve, wait on, minister to..". Depending on it's context, that word can describe the ministry of a priest (Ex 28:35) and worshiping God. Deut 18:5 And as a participle, "servant, minister..." p1560 NIV Study Bible

From that explanation of the word *Sarat,* it is obvious that the words 'servant' and 'minister', are virtually the same. That close connection between those two words, ties in with how Jesus defined his ministry. He said,

 "the Son of Man did not come to be served; he came to serve...." Mark 10:35 GN

And that is how Jesus would like each Christian to see themselves, as servants or ministers - and when our life is finished, he would love to be able to say to each of us.

"Well done, good and faithful servant." Matt 25:21 NIV

Those two words, servants and ministers, define the role of Christians on Earth, and I suspect, in heaven as well. When we get to heaven, I don't think we will spend eternity, strumming harps and jumping from, cloud to cloud. The angels who are already there, are servants or ministers.

Down on Earth, the Church can only function because disciples of Jesus consider themselves to be; servants or ministers. I don't know of any Church that has an oil rig out the back of it's property, pumping out oil so that the Church can pay people in the congregation to do a variety of tasks including: welcoming people   at the door, teaching children, playing musical instruments etc.

The words 'servant' or 'minister', defines our role as Christians, but let's think about those words for a few pages, because I have yet to read in secular literature, the merits of being, a servant minister.

For example, High Schools, students are not offered courses that emphasise the value of living a serving or ministering life-style. And apart from the education system, the values of the advertising industry, shape what people value and spend their time and money on.

   The   implicit message in many adverts, is this.

> *When you buy this product, you will be happy.*

Rubbish! Our lives might be 3% easier doing a particular task, if we buy the   product advertised, but buying that product or any product, will only us give a temporary blimp of happiness. Only a blimp,   because that happiness is all to do with self – so ultimately, it is not, real happiness.

So rather than buying into the message that,

happiness is found by pandering to our self through buying this or that - ditch it in favour of the mindset of Jesus. Happiness is found in looking at the interests of others and building the kingdom of God.

Because the value of being a servant minister is not promoted in   our high schools or secular society, following on are some reasons to value, being a servant minister.

<u>The value of being a servant minister, like Jesus</u>

(1) Servant ministers change individuals, society and the kingdom of God, for good. Those concerned solely with the kingdom of me, may change themselves in some way, more likely for their own comfort and pleasure or standing in the eyes of others.

(2) It is implicit in what Paul wrote about being ministers of the Gospel, that he thought it was a 'privilege' to be a servant or minister of the Gospel. That it was an honour to serve, the King of Kings! Phil 3:7-11

That thought is also implicit in a word he used in his second letter to the Church at Corinth. Paul wrote, we are, "ambassadors" of Christ. 2 Cor 5:20

An ambassador is not like an ordinary citizen who lives for a period of time in another country.   An ambassador has the 'privilege' of representing his or her country, just as we have the privilege of representing King Jesus, in a world whose values we do not always share.

In using the word servant, perhaps it is necessary to distinguish between the role and the position, of a servant. A servant in Jesus' time and today, is a lowly position. But what is important, is the mind-set of a servant. I.e. It is possible to be a CEO or a King or Queen, and have a servant mindset.

A CEO or monarch who has a servant mindset, will be in authority over many people but, they will not be focussed on the importance of their position; rather, their mission, as a servant leader.

(3) The   goal of most Christians, is to follow in the footsteps of Jesus, and consequently be, a serving ministering person. A serving/ministering person may do, any of the following.

Give, heal, lead, encourage, pray for, stand by, console, mentor, organise, sympathise, counsel, advise, serve, assist, facilitate, reconcile and bless.

Each of those words,   describe the actions of a servant/minister. .

In promoting the servant/minister life-style, for some   that   will not be appealing – possibly because of a mindset. A mindset that a life of ministering to others and building the kingdom, will be a life of drudgery!

There is a joy in a life of ministry and serving, in the here and now, which comes from the Holy Spirit. Not a high-five type of joy or happiness, but a deep, constant; and   lasting type of joy or happiness.

When the people of Israel were back in the land of Israel after their exile in Babylon and while they were in the process of rebuilding the city of Jerusalem,   their   leader   Nehemiah urged them not to weep. He said, "the joy of the Lord is your strength."

After the disciples returned from ministering in the villages of Judea, they returned in joy. Luke 10:17

(4) A 'giving, serving, ministering' person never thinks of getting anything back, when they give, serve or minister. A serving/ministering person only thinks of, the good of the others, or the Church or the kingdom of God - but I have noticed.

Sooner or later, either those served or maybe even others who were not served, have noticed the serving/ministering disciple, and will try to find a way to express their appreciation - and maybe even give something, in return.

It may be as small as a smile or word of thanks or it may even be something more tangible.

A servants or ministering life-style is like having an interest-bearing bank account. An interest accrues in the bank account of those who have a kingdom mentality and an account called; *minister and servant of Christ.*

The rest of this book draws on further insights

from Jesus' ministry. Those insights help us define our ministry in Jerusalem (our immediate area), Judea (our local area), or Samaria (out of the local area and comfort zone); and to the ends of the Earth. C.f. Acts 1:8

Chapter 2

His definitions – our model

Let's begin reviewing the "I have come... statements, Jesus made. Jesus did not begin his ministry and then seek to find, reasons for it. From well before the start of his ministry, Jesus knew exactly what he wanted to achieve, why he wanted to achieve it and how.

Jesus said, "for I have not come to call the righteous, but sinners." Matt 9.13 What scandalised the religious teachers of his time, was that Jesus, mixed with sinners. Much more is written about this subject in the chapter called, 'Other religious groups in

Israel', but for now, this purpose,   has been noted.

Jesus said, "For the Son of Man came to seek and to save what was lost." Luke 19.10 One of the express purposes Jesus came, was to seek out and save the lost. There were two verbs in that quote from Jesus. The first verb being, "seek" and the second being "save". The first verb implies that Jesus' attitude, was not.

'They are lost. They were foolish. They did not take a GPS locator beacon with them or consult maps before they left. Because they did not take appropriate measures to ensure they would not get lost or be located. They have to bear full responsibility for being lost. It is not concern or problem.'

That was not Jesus attitude, at all. He cared about people who were lost; what-ever the reason.   That is why we read about Jesus inviting himself to the house of a "lost" tax collector called Zaachaeus.

I suspect Jesus reasoned. Those who were lost, had become disorientated by the many options they had and the conflicting advice - and as a result of being unsure about which route to take to take to find life happiness and life; and who to listen to - they had become, disorientated and then lost.

As for being lost, what did Jesus mean by the word? The word is usually used to describe someone lost in a remote area, or a child that has become separated from it's parent/s – but there are plenty of lost adults as well a children and it is not necessary to be in a remote area, to be lost.

There are plenty of people who are lost who live in urban areas. That fact is epitomised by the words on the T shirt of a man who appeared to be in his early to mid 20's, and was waiting at a bus stop in a big city. His dress was smart, but casual. On his T-shirt were the words,

I AM STILL LOST.

Full marks for his honesty.

When Jesus used the word "lost", was he meaning that many people who had homes and addresses and work and life-styles, were lost? Almost certainly. It is also implicit in what Jesus said:

> (a) Many who are lost, do not know they are lost.

> (b) Some knew they were lost, but did not the way out or even what home looked like, so they could make their way home.

Jesus called wealthy Zaachaeus "lost." He

was lost, but did not know it. He had bought a tax collecting franchise knowing that the pay was minimal, but the Romans who sold these tax-collecting franchises, sold them to the franchisees with the understanding.

"We want you to collect the taxes the citizens owe us; and if you happen to collect a little extra on the side, we will turn a blind eye."

The word "little" was never defined, so tax collectors like Zaachaeus, habitually collected extra.

The Romans knew it. The tax collectors knew it and the citizens who were taxed, knew it. Everyone knew that a tax collector would collect extra above what he was required to pay the Romans, and the only person who would determine the amount to be collected, was the tax collector.

Citizens also knew that if they refused to pay what the tax collector demanded, the tax collector could threaten them with a visit from Roman soldiers, who, not being Jews; probably treated the visit as something like henchmen of a mobster
 would treat one of his clients, who was not paying up.

Zaachaeus had intentionally bought this tax collecting   franchise; knowing it was unpopular but saw it as   a less   than scrupulous way,   to   get-rich, and by implication; find significance and happiness.

In Jesus view, he was "lost", because for he was seeking importance and happiness; from wealth.

I was interested in a non-Christian reporters view of As Vegas. A summary of her views was this. There was plenty of glitz and glamour in the city, but when she looked in the eyes of people of the city, they looked dead. She called them, "the living dead".

And perhaps that is what Jesus saw in Zaachaeus. A man who had a good income stream and a home, but was perhaps in Jesus view, "the living dead."

After Jesus had invited himself to Zaachaeus home and Zaachaeus had said that he was prepared to repay those he had defrauded. Jesus said,

 "Salvation has come to this house...", Luke 19:1-9

Jesus used the word "lost", to describe wealthy people like Zaachaeus. He also used the word "lost", to describe the prodigal son. The prodigal son tried to find happiness and life in; endless parties and prostitutes.

Jesus recognised that both were lost, but

cared about these lost people who were seeking life and happiness in the wrong place, and in the wrong way.

Building on what Jesus said, we can say that. Anyone, whether they live in a slum or are included in the *Forbes Fortune 500 rich list* - are lost; as is, everyone in between. Anyone who has not made Jesus their Lord, and the kingdom of God, their absolute priority, in life.

Some burdens, Jesus would like to take from us such as guilt about past sins or mistakes. Other burdens he would like us to pick up, such as the burden had for the lost people of his time, and still has for the lost, in our time.

Jesus' statement about coming to seek and save the lost, ties in with another his, "I have come..." saying.   He said, "I have come that they might have life, and have it to the full." John 10:10 NIV

Jesus offered five things to those who became his disciples. Eternal life when this life is finished, and our other precious commodities during our life on Earth. Commodities that the lost are seeking. Jesus offered his disciples, a sense of being valued, peace, happiness and life.

Those last four, are usually what lost people are seeking, except that they seek those things, in ways that will never truly provide them. Through drugs and alcohol. Personal relationships, sports, causes, success, creativity, recreational life-styles, philosophy, and various religions etc.

To Jesus, those four desires (to feel valued, to find peace, happiness and life) are only truly found in a relationship to God our creator and being united with himself. Through being full of the Holy Spirit and through serving and ministering to others.

Jesus' mission statement

The "I have come...'statements define our ministry. Jesus, mission statement, also defines our ministry. In his mission statement, found in Luke chapter 4, the first line is. "The Spirit of the Lord is on me..."

It is both the Old Testament and New Testaments, we find the same theme. We need the Holy Spirit, to build the kingdom of God.

Before he started his ministry, Elisha asked for a double portion of the Holy Spirit. The prophet Zechariah when speaking about rebuilding the walls of Jerusalem, said, "Not by might, nor by power, but by my Spirit... Zech 4:6

David, author of the majority of the Psalms, wrote. "The Spirit of the Lord, spoke through me...2 Sam 23:2 NIV

Paul, writing to the Christians at Ephesus, wrote. "Be filled with the Spirit." When the Apostle Paul wrote to the Christians at Ephesus "be filled with the Spirit", his words were in the present tense, continuous.

Jesus waited until he was anointed by the Holy Spirit, before beginning his ministry and before the first disciples began their ministry, Jesus urged the disciples to "wait" for the Holy Spirit.

The first line of Jesus' mission-statement emphasises that whatever our ministry in or contribution to, the kingdom of God, we (all 1.8 billion of us), need the help of the Holy Spirit.

Our relationship to the Holy Spirit is like some functions we attend. Some functions are 'INVITATION ONLY'. It is the same with the Holy Spirit. He awaits our invitation. The Holy Spirit will come and fill our lives, but we have to invite him, preferably, each day.

The subsequent lines of Jesus' mission statement state that Jesus was anointed "because" and "to" ...

- "preach",

- "proclaim",

- "recover sight",

- "release"

All of these activities, tie in with Jesus' goal of serving and ministering. They are also remind us that the Holy Spirit comes for both our personal benefit (i.e. the fruits of love and joy and peace and patience and kindness), and to assist us in ministry.

One of the key goals of the Holy Spirit, is to make each Christian like, a water conduit. A conduit   through which   life-giving water, flows into, parched lands.

Moving on further with Jesus'   mission statement, he spoke of "setting prisoners free". Here there is a problem in that we have no record of Jesus visiting   any jails,   and setting prisoners free. So what did he mean?

The answer is not straight forward because, Jesus was quoting Isaiah, so it is necessary to ask.

(a) What did Isaiah mean, by those words?

(b) What did Jesus mean, when he quoted
    Isaiah's words?

(c) What do Jesus' words, mean for us?

What Isaiah meant, is a separate study. What did Jesus mean by setting prisoners free, we can only speculate about - but can speculate with concrete examples, from his ministry.

Setting prisoners free

Maybe Jesus meant freedom from bondage to the religious system which had over a thousand laws to obey - see chapter 6 – *Other religious groups in Israel*. Jesus accused the Pharisees of loading the people with heavy burdens, burdens they could scarcely carry. Luke 11:46 By contrast, Jesus created a religion that was simplified and easy to apply.

 Or freedom from sin? Jesus said he had come to give his life as a ransom (Mark 10:45), and a ransom is a sum of money paid to free a person from debt. So maybe Jesus meant he had come to set people free from the guilt and bondage of sin?

Or freedom from the god of money? Matt 6:24 Jesus spoke of people who "serve" the god of money. Some wealthy people, or even people who don't have a lot of money, but desire it; think that money will give them life and happiness.

Having ample spare money is freeing in the sense of not having to worry about how to pay the bills. But some people with ample spare money, end up, 'serving' money.

When that has occurred, it has become like a god they serve, and they never seem to have enough, even though they already have plenty by most others, standard. When that has occurred, money has   become, in Jesus words, their "master" and Jesus came to free people, from the god of money.

Or did Jesus mean he had come to free people from resentment towards others. Jesus taught his disciples to forgive those who had wronged them because he recognised that people can become, prisoners of their own, resentment. Matt 18:22.

Essentially Jesus was saying. It is freeing to forgive others. By forgiving others, a person unbinds the chains that tie them to the person or persons who wronged them. By forgiving others; it does not mean that what they did was right. If just means that the wronged person is no longer bound, by the other persons wrong doing.

Or did Jesus mean, freedom from hate? Some people of his time, hated the Romans.

Jesus taught disciples to love, even their enemies. In fact he urged his disciples to go the second mile for them. Luke 6:27

Or did Jesus mean, freedom from demonic powers or sickness? Matt 8:1-4 Both sickness and demons, bound their prisoners.

Or did Jesus mean, freedom from the fear of death? Jesus spoke words of reassurance to those worried about what would happen, when they died. John 14:1-3.His opening words were. "Do not let your hearts be troubled." NLT

He did so again to one of the thieves on the cross. Jesus words to the thief who was also dying, were. "I assure you, today you will be with me in Paradise." Luke 23:43 NLT

Or did Jesus mean, freedom from poverty? Matt 25:35 Jesus said that whenever a disciple gives to those who are hungry or thirsty, they are, in a sense; giving to him.

- - - - - - - -

We are not told what Jesus meant when he quoted the prophet Isaiah about setting prisoners free. It is likely that Jesus meant, all of these freedoms, and more.

The Spirit of the Lord was on Jesus to set

people free. The same Spirit is on us, to set people free from, every type of prison. Fear of poverty, from false gods, wealth, religious systems, the fear of death, the guilt of sin, demonic powers, unforgiveness and hate.

Continuing with Jesus' mission statement, it speaks of recovery of sight, to the blind. In a number of statements, Jesus implied that some people of his time; were spiritually blind. He quoted the prophet Isaiah saying. ..you will be ever seeing but never perceiving." Matt 13:14 NIV

We also know that he restored sight to the physically blind such as blind Bartimaeus. Mark 10:46-52. So what did Jesus mean by his words "the blind will see?" Almost certainly he meant both the physically blind, and the spiritually blind.

Jesus' mission statement continues. ...to proclaim the year of the Lord's favour. Jesus knew that his coming, was synonymous with a time of God's special favour for the people of this Earth. At his birth, the angels sang, ''and on earth peace to men on whom his favour rests." Luke 2:14 NIV

Many of the Old Testament prophets predicted a future time of the God's special favour to the people of Israel. "The day is coming..." said the prophet Jeremiah in Jeremiah 31:27. Then four verses later when speaking about the new covenant with the people of Israel, Jeremiah repeated that same phrase, "The day is coming..."

Simeon who was at the Temple, recognised that when he saw the baby Jesus, the time of the Lord's favour - the day had come!

And when Jesus began his ministry, he said. "Repent, for the kingdom of heaven is near".Matt 4:17 NIV

Many people must have made the connection between what Jesus was saying and doing; and what was foretold by prophets like Jeremiah. The time of the Lord's favour, had finally come.

His "I have come..." sayings define our ministry. So does his mission statement, and even the "I am..." sayings do, because they remind us, who to direct people to. Jesus!

Jesus the gate, Jesus the way, Jesus the truth, Jesus the life and Jesus, the resurrection.

If people are looking for the gateway to God, direct them to Jesus. If they are looking for the truth, direct them to Jesus. If the are looking for life, direct them to Jesus. If they are looking for certainty about life beyond this life, direct them to Jesus.

- - - - - - - -

All the other books in this 'Jesus series', contribute to the picture of Jesus' ministry. This book identifies the nature and features of his ministry. The book *The Son,* identifies the personal qualities, Jesus brought to his ministry. The book *The Incarnation of Jesus,* emphasises that his was an, incarnational ministry. The book *Jesus changed our lives* is about the impact Jesus made to the lives of people, mentioned in that book.

34 His definitions – our model

What Jesus did

Chapter 3

An image of his ministry

The first two chapters of this book revolved around what Jesus *said,* most of the following chapters revolve around what Jesus *did*! A special feature about what Jesus said, and what he did; were one and the same. See the final chapter of the book, *The Son.*

We see Jesus doing that with prayer. He taught his disciples to pray and how to pray and what to pray for. With prayer, Jesus, like his other teachings, walked his talk. During his ministry, Jesus frequently called head office. His Father in heaven.

- Very early in the morning, while it was still dark, Jesus got up, left the house and went off to a solitary place, where he prayed. Mark 1:35

- One day, Jesus was praying in a certain place. Luke 11:1

- 'After he had dismissed them, he went up on a mountainside by himself to pray'. Matt 14:23

Jesus prayed before all of the significant phases of his ministry. Before the start of his ministry. Luke 4:2. Before the selection of his disciples. Luke 6:12 and before his trial and crucifixion. Luke 11:41

But what other features, were characteristic of Jesus ministry? In the books of the 'Jesus Series', I attempted to take a fresh look at him. because there are so few books about him- apart from those who want to paint him as a revolutionary or a zealot.

 As I looked afresh at the ministry of Jesus in the Gospels, something hit me about the three years of his ministry. They were largely;

relationship, relationship, relationship!

Many times during his ministry, Jesus sat around a table, eating, drinking and enjoying the hospitality of others. Matt 9.9, 12.1-2,

Luke 7.36, 11.37, 19.1-9, 22.7-23, Mark 7.1-4, John 12.1-11.

Jesus admitted that he was perceived as a 'glutton' and a 'drunkard' (or winebibber K.J) Luke 7.34. The Jews of his of his day associated being religious with a serious face (like the Pharisees), and staying, well away from sinful people. Or that being religious meant to live like John the Baptist and dressing in sheep skins, and conducting your ministry, in a remote spot.

Some may have held the impression that to be truly religious, meant living in a strict religious community, where sinners were banned – such as the Essene community.

Jesus was so different to these groups. He was passionately religious, but he spent time with people and was available to people, who approached him, anywhere. Many times it was at a meal table, and other times, on the road. The expression, "on the road" is found 32 times in Luke's Gospel.

with the twelve disciples, there was this same emphasis on relationships When he called the disciples, he did not give them a folder containing his teachings and say to them. "If you want to consider becoming one of my disciples,   go away and study these teachings. Then, if you are happy with my teachings, you can come back and ask to become a disciple of mine."

Nor did Jesus give them a twelve point plan on how he was going to conduct his ministry so they could consider that also. A plan that included all the relevant information such as. When, where, how and who, would arrange his public meetings. And how frequently they would have, group training sessions.

When Jesus began to assemble a group of disciples, he gave them no details about his plans for his ministry or what his teachings were. All he said to the first disciples was.

"Come. Follow me…"

What was important to Jesus was that the disciples develop a relationship with himself first, then understand the mission later.

It is worth noting, that Jesus still calls people today, the same way. When Jesus called Saul of Tarsus from heaven; he did not appear to him on the Damascus road and say. "Saul of Tarsus you are hurting my teachings or you are hurting my Church (which he was). Jesus said, "you are hurting Me."

Paul would never forget the fact that it was Jesus who called him to follow him. And it is the same with each person. Jesus knocks on the door of their life; asking to be let in so he can come and have, "fellowship" with us.

Jesus' invitation to "come follow me" was not the normal way of creating a team of disciples, in those times. There were other teachers (Rabbi's) around who had disciples, but they only became disciples   after they had asked the Rabbi, if they could follow the Rabbai.

Then the Rabbi would consider their request for a while. Perhaps ask them to think through his teachings, and usually prove in some way that they would be worthy disciples. Then hopefully,   the Rabbi would agree to their becoming a disciple.

Jesus ignored the normal process and came to fishermen and a tax collector where they worked, and asked them to follow him.

I sometimes wonder what we would have said if Jesus came to our office or farm or factory or home and simply said, "would you come and follow me?"

Jesus created a band of disciples by inviting them to form an ever-growing relationship with himself. And it was during three years of forming an ever-growing relationship with him, that they learnt about his' teachings and purposes. The only specifics Jesus gave the fishermen disciples (when he called them), was that they were to become, fishers of men and women.

During the next three years, after accepting Jesus' invitation, the first disciples followed Jesus over the hillsides - and besides the Sea of Galilee. They followed him into various towns, and to Jerusalem, the Capital city.

They observed him in various homes. The homes of the disciples. The homes of the Pharisees, and even the home of a despised tax collector. They were with Jesus around meal tables and by the sea shore, and in a boat during a storm.

They watched and listened as he debated with the Pharisees. Talked with a Samaritan woman at a well, and picked up children. They saw him heal a leper, a blind person; and another time, someone who was deaf and mute. They noted how, demons fled at his command.

During those three years of relationship-building, the disciples asked Jesus questions about prayer and faith and suffering and the end times.

By the end of those three years, we see the impact on the disciples, of all that relationship-building. There was a love between Jesus and his disciples shown at the last supper by the way John leaned on his chest, and all the disciples, bar one, said they were prepared to die for him.

Out of his growing relationship with the disciples, Jesus developed a love for them, and they for him. At the end of his ministry, Jesus said. "I have called you friends,…" John 15:15 (N.I.V.)

The goal of the relationship-building, was that Jesus and the disciples become "one", just as he and the Father were "one"'. John 17:22

The value Jesus placed on love relationships, is illustrated by his conversation with Peter, after Jesus' resurrection. During that conversation, Jesus asked Peter three times, "Do you love me?"

 It is highly likely Jesus asked that question, three times – to remind Peter of the three times he had denied Jesus.

The amazing part about those questions is that Jesus did pour scorn on Peter and say.

"Peter, aren't you ashamed that you denied me before two mere servant girls and another person - particularly since you insisted at the last supper that you were prepared to die for me!"

Two significant words in that question (repeated three times) are the words, "love" and "me". Those two words characterize the new religion Jesus founded.

It was a completely new way of starting a new religious movement but method of building a new religious movement, was always going to have it's problems because, relationships are not always, simple.

In a real relationship with other people, the relationship soon progresses beyond the "its great to see you" stage, and talking about the weather and how they act and react in different situations.

 As people spend more time with each other, both parties get to know the other beyond the surface level, and what their values are.

Because Jesus set out to build a close relationship with the first disciples, he saw the best of them, and their possibilities, but also their worst. The disciples shooed children away, whom mothers had brought to Jesus, so he could bless them. They tried to stop another person delivering people from the power of Satan, because that person was not 'one of them' . The 'in-crowd'.

Two disciples asked Jesus if they could call down fire from heaven on those who would not allow him into their village and they argued about, who would have the best position next to Jesus, in heaven. And when things really mattered, they went to sleep in the garden of Gethsemane!

So by the time Jesus finally commissioned the disciples to take the Gospel into all the World* before his ascent into heaven, Jesus had become 'very familiar' with both their strengths, and weaknesses.

*Matt 28:19

It is amazing that, in spite of being aware of their failings, Jesus commissioned the first disciples to be the leaders of the new Church.

Given their record of selfish desires, why would Jesus entrust the future of the Church, into their hands? Was it because, as a result of three years of relationship building, Jesus came to believe in them, and love them?

It is implicit in the Gospel record that he believed in them and explicit that he loved them. Also, Jesus knew that after the Holy Spirit came on them; these scared rabbits - these broken shards of pottery; would be transformed into vessels fit to be called, "Apostles."

Do you see what occurred during those three years of relationship building? Both parties came to believe in each other. The disciples came to believe Jesus was the 'Son of God', and Jesus came to believe that these, at times selfish, at times blind disciples could be and would be fit leaders of the new Church.

This exchange of belief, is amply illustrated by two conversations Jesus had with Peter. Before his death and resurrection. Peter had come to recognise that Jesus was the Son of God, and told Jesus so. See the conversation found in Matt 16:16.

At that time, Peter was saying in effect to Jesus. I believe in you. You are not merely a carpenter from Nazareth. You are the Son of God!

Then after his resurrection, it was Jesus turn

to say to Peter, I believe in you. Jesus should have poured scorn on Peter at that time for doing what he said he would not do. At the last supper Peter said that even if the others betrayed Jesus, he would not and was prepared to die for Jesus.

Then during the trial, Peter swore that he did not now Jesus, three times – before a mere servant girl. So when they met after Jesus' resurrection, Jesus had every reason to condemn Peter.

Instead of scorn, Jesus' words were in effect. Peter, I still believe in you. We can conclude that because at that time Jesus commissioned Peter to be the head of the Church. i.e. Jesus said to him, "feed my lambs" and "feed my sheep."

I hope readers get the connection. Jesus would like us to say to him. "I believe in you Jesus. You are the Son of God." In turn, Jesus wants us to hear his words.

"I believe in you Be all you can be, in my name!"

Apart from the twelve, we can see the same emphasis on relationships with the other disciples. When Mary and Martha sent an urgent message to Jesus that their brother was very ill, the words we read in John's Gospel tell us a lot about Jesus' relationship with that family.

"Lord the one you love is sick."

 Jesus loved Martha, Mary and Lazarus, for he said.

 "Our friend Lazarus has fallen asleep.", John 11: 3-11(N.I.V.)

The word (friend) implies that, Jesus had spent many hours at the home of Mary, Martha and Lazarus. When Lazarus died, Martha reminded Jesus of his love for Lazarus. The Apostle John, was only stating what he had observed when he wrote

> "Jesus loved Martha and her sister
> and Lazarus...." John 11:5(N.I.V.)

When Jesus wanted to evangelize Zacchaeus, the cheating tax-collector, he did not give him a tract, or lambaste him for his obvious sins, but said in effect - "I am coming to your house, for a meal."

Dining with sinners was completely opposite to the tack both the Pharisees and Essenes took. The Pharisees kept themselves apart from sinners like Zaachaeus, while the Essenes took a further step. They separated themselves completely from all sinners; and lived in a remote, righteous community.

Even though this is only the first image of Jesus' ministry, in this book, there must be something in this image of Jesus' ministry that applies to the way we do Church today. If church is largely a series of rituals or well defined programs, the Church has lost it's way.

To Jesus, religion is at best, a series of relationships. A relationship with the Father, Son and the Holy Spirit. A love relationship with our self. A love relationships with fellow disciples and with the people of our community. Wherever people are found, on the face of the globe.

 There is another angle to the effort Jesus put into establishing a close relationship with the first disciples. Although this book is primarily about Jesus during his three years of ministry, he has not changed. The emphatic statement of the author of the book of Hebrews, is.

Jesus Christ is the same, yesterday, today and forever. Hebrews 13:8.

 The 'same' Jesus who developed a love relationship with the first disciples, wants a love relationship with you and I today. His goal is to be, and to quote his own words. "I in them....John 17:23

Or consider the words Jesus spoke to the Apostle John in a vision.

> "Look I stand at the door and knock. If you hear my voice and open the door I will come in, and we will share a meal together as friends" Rev 3:20 (NLT)

 With the first disciples, Jesus was well aware that they were not perfect when he called them and they revealed, further weaknesses, while under training. But this 'same' Jesus, calls us on the same basis.

He does not demand perfection from any person   before knocking of our life or any person's life; asking to be let in.

And once he has been invited in. He knows that we, like the first disciples, will   make mistakes, along the way as our selfish desires come to the surface or we deny Jesus or go to sleep in the job.

Despite knowing that we can and will make mistakes, he comes knocking so that he can have fellowship with us; in the hope that out of the on-going relationship with him, we begin to change into his likeness.

Further,   Jesus' example of mixing with all sorts of people means he wants, you and I, to do the same. To   be Gospel lights in the Church. At our work-place or home or place of study. In the factory or on the farm or in the office. At social events and sports events.

Gospel lights to those struggling with issues and struggling to making ends meet, and to those who seem to have it all together, and have it all. To the religious, and the not so religious. To the sick and the well. The young and the old.   Where ever people are; who ever they are.

His example is our model.

With the Father and Holy Spirit

Jesus not only had a close relationship with his disciples – but he also an incredibly close relationship   with   his   heavenly   Father. Speaking about that relationship, he said "I and the Father are one." John 10:30

If the strength of relationships could be measured and quantified, there could be, 6 categories.

- Non existent

- Distant

- Good

- Close

- Very close

- Totally-one. (i.e. both parties have achieved oneness)

Jesus had the last, a totally-one relationship, with his Heavenly Father. Further he said

> "my nourishment comes from doing the will of God who sent me". John 4:34(NLT)

What Jesus consumed, and in a sense, what consumed Jesus, was the will of His Father in Heaven. That is how close he was to His Heavenly Father.

Jesus also had a close relationship with the Holy Spirit. The late Dr Derek Prince has pointed out that many New Testament references to the Holy Spirit, in the original Greek, were rendered in the more personal "Holy Spirit", and not " the Holy Spirit."

It was as a result of his close relationship with Holy Spirit, that Jesus was led into the wilderness. Matt 4:1

My picture of the occasion when Holy Spirit led Jesus into the wilderness, as being similar to a friend, taking us by the shoulder, and leading us to another place, because that friend has our good, in mind.

After his time of testing in the desert, Luke records that he returned to Galilee, 'in the power of the Spirit,' Luke 4:14(N.I.V.) His friend, Holy Spirit, had led Jesus back out of the desert,

 When the seventy two disciples returned from a missionary trip, Luke wrote. 'At that time Jesus, full of joy through the Holy Spirit,...Luke 10:21 (N.I.V.)   Later in his ministry, Jesus talked to the disciples about his friend - Holy Spirit. Jesus said, "It is for your good that I go, if I do not go, the Counsellor* will not come". *meaning Holy Spirit.

It is implied by these words that Jesus and Holy Spirit were working in tandem to create the Church. Jesus to lay the foundation, and Holy Spirit to come afterwards, and build on that foundation. I.e. To work in tandem means there is a relationship of trust and confidence in each other.

It was out of his relationships of oneness with Holy Spirit and with the Father, and his relationships with the early disciples, that the bricks and mortar of the early Church, were laid.

In John chapter seventeen, Jesus prayed for the disciples. Among the relationships he prayed for were;

Jesus and the disciples would be "one"

Jesus would be 'in' them

The disciples would be "in" Jesus.

The disciples would be "in" the world

Chapter 4

The Everywhere Church

There is a French medical aid agency called **Medicins Sans Frontieres,** which roughly translated means 'Medicines without borders'. Looking at the three years of Jesus' ministry, he created an Ekklesia Sans Frontieres – a Church without walls'.

Speaking about the kingdom of God Jesus said, people will not be able to say, "Here it is or there it is..." Luke 17:21 NIV Meaning there are no borders or walls, to the kingdom of God.

In the Church without walls, Jesus dined in

the homes of his disciples like Martha and Mary, the homes of enquiring Pharisees and the homes of obvious sinners like, Zacchaeus - the tax collector.

Once he was teaching in a home, when the roof began to fall in because friends of a lame man, desperate to get their friend to Jesus, began to break away the roof of the building. When I picture that scene, I wonder whether there was a smile on Jesus' face as bits of roof began to fall onto the floor beside him, and perhaps because he was a carpenter - he made a joke about the poor construction skills of the builders?

NB While keeping an eye on the page you are reading, please turn to the cover of this book for a moment and take a look at Jesus. He is smiling. I suggest he smiled a lot during his ministry. It is just that the times he smiled, are not recorded in the Gospels.

Whether the fact the Gospel writers did not mention the number of times he smiled is because of the prohibition against images found in the book of Numbers, I am not sure. However, without any evidence to back it up, I am sure that Jesus smiled a lot.

To return to the scene in the house where the

roof was being pulled back by people, desperate to get the lame man to Jesus.

Often his Church was the home of people. Or the streets of towns, or the roads, linking towns. On roads, all sorts of people met him. The leader of a Synagogue. Representatives of a Roman Centurion. Ten lepers. Bartimaeus, the blind man. A woman with an incurable condition. A Samaritan woman who was in her fifth relationship with a man.

His pulpit varied. Sometimes it was the hillsides of Galilee. Other times it was in a boat moored, not far from the shore. Sometimes his pulpit was a meal table - that of Mary and Martha, or a Pharisee, or Zaachaeus house.

 And the last supper was in the upper room of a house – and the Gospel writers offer us no clue who house it was. whether it belonged to a disciple or someone interested in the ministry of Jesus, but not a disciple? .

There must be a message for the Church today, from Jesus' model of ministry! I think the message is this.

Though the central act of our faith, is the service of worship in the Church building. The Church   is best represented by each

Christian, viewing their homes as part of the Church, without walls.

Their business or place of employment; as part of the Church, without walls. A sports or social club or ministry in the community as part of, the Church without walls.

Sometimes our actions at these various locations may seem insignificant, but in the economy of the kingdom of God, even small actions are incredibly significant - are of, incredible worth.

Jesus indicated the significance and the value of small acts in the kingdom of God, when he said. "If anyone gives you even a cup of water because you belong to the Messiah, I tell you the truth, that person shall surely be rewarded." Mark 9:41 NLT

Through these words, it is as if Jesus is saying.

> If our lives are a series of seemingly insignificant words and actions. Prayers prayed, words of truth or kindness or encouragement spoken. Acts of kindness and service and thoughtfulness.

> Each of these small actions create a symphony of praise to our heavenly

father and from heavens perspective, makes us like the brightest star in the sky - in the Church without walls.

Sometimes there is a mindset among Christians - to 'serve the Lord and be truly Christian, I must be in some kind of full time or part-time work in a Church or Christian organization.

Jesus still calls Christians to serve him, full or part-time   in Churches and   Christian ministries. But the ministry Jesus modelled, means, he rejoices over each Christian living for him, anywhere on the planet, we   call Earth. And because the church has no walls, everywhere the Christian goes, becomes the Church.

<u>The anytime Church</u>

To help Christians plan their week, each Church has a set day and time for worship. Though the overall outline of Jesus' ministry was planned and he had set goals, much of it was spontaneous! Whether that was caused by individuals approaching him in the street, or Jesus taking advantage of an opportunity that arose.

When Jesus returned to his base in Capernaum, he recognised that the disciples had been arguing over who was the greatest, so Jesus took advantage of the fact there was a child in the house who was familiar with Jesus, and stood the child in front of the disciples, then said

> "Whoever welcomes this little child in my name, welcomes me...Luke 9.46-48

It has been pointed out that in Luke's Gospel, 32 times there is the expression "along the way". Meaning, during one of his journeys, "along the way", Jesus stopped and paid attention to a person or a group of people he had encountered.

Along the way, a Synagogue ruler approached him and representatives of a Roman Centurion. Along the way, ten lepers met him, and along the way, blind Bartimaeus called out as he passed by.

Along the way, a woman with an incurable condition reached out to touch him, and along the way; and Jesus stopped to talk to a Samaritan woman, who was in her sixth relationship with a man.

The point about Jesus response to people he met along the way, is that people were more important to Jesus, than his schedule.

A sign I read in a shop that was addressed to employees, reiterates that point.

> 'Customers are not here to interrupt your day, they are the reason for your day.'

Likewise, most people we meet during the course of our day, are the reason for our day.

A church service takes place at a set address and at a set time/s. Churches may be at fixed addresses and times, but Jesus' disciples are not restricted to any of these. Anywhere, any time, is okay to bring the Church to any person or group of persons. .

 An example from my life. When I worked as a supervisor at bus company, with up to 140 drivers to manage, and buses to keep running and computer records to be maintained – the office was busy.

Further, our company was contracted to the city council and required to keep our buses running on time, or face a reasonably high fine from the city council, particularly   if any buses ran over 30 minutes late.

But human lives do not always fit in with company schedules. One day I received a phone call from a family member to say that the husband of one of our female bus driver's husband, had been rushed to hospital, with a serious heart condition.

At that point, it was important to both, maintain the bus service on schedule, if at all possible; and   get the female employee, to her husband's side.

After discussion, it was agreed another employee would take a company car and try and meet the female driver along her scheduled route. Once that plan was agreed on, I called her over the r/t to tell her that another driver would meet her along the route and complete her trip, and asked her to return to the depot in the company car, so she could go and be with her husband.

That phone call interrupted the smooth flow of more easily dealt-with problems and issues. But that phone-call wasn't an interruption to my day. Rather, it was the reason for my position and one of the reasons, for my day.

Chapter 5

Clearing the Temple

Mark 11:15-17

The way Jesus cleared the Temple of traders with a whip, is an image that seems, so at odds with other images of Jesus. Jesus healing people. Jesus holding children. Jesus teaching people, or gathering wheat husks in his hand as he and disciples, walked along.

Napoleon Bonaparte reportedly said "if Jesus had not existed, we never would have been able to create him." I think Napoleon was meaning, the various images of Jesus are so different, including; using a whip, to clear the traders from the Temple.

The story of the clearing of the temple is important to us today in a number of ways. Although Christians by nature of their calling, desire to heal people. To help people and reconcile them to others, and to God. There were times in both Testaments when God's people, chose to please God, rather than comply with the expectations of their rulers, or their fellow citizens.

And when they did not comply with these expectations, it usually did not go down well. Feathers became ruffled and sometimes scorn was poured on those who decided, God's values, mattered most.

For example, after Jesus ascended to heaven, Peter and the other Apostles were instructed not to preach about Jesus, by the Sanhedrin. The Sanhedrin (the ruling religious council) had the power to order Jews to comply with their wishes. However, Peter and John refused to be bound by the Sanhedrin's instruction that they should not preach about Jesus. Peter and John said in effect "... we must obey God rather than men." Acts 4:19

Peter and John were not alone. The Apostle Paul wrote

"Do not conform any longer to the

pattern of this World…. ” Rom 12:2
(N.I.V.)

The prophets of the Old Testament also were often at odds with the political and religious rulers of their time. So Jesus' actions in the Temple, were consistent with God's people throughout the Bible

The reasons for Jesus clearing the Temple courtyard of it's traders and money-changers, appear to be two-fold.

1. He was no longer prepared to see poor pilgrims pay exorbitant (monopoly) prices for the animals they were required to buy as sacrifices, and

2. Pilgrims from other countries, had to pay an exorbitant exchange-rate for their foreign currency.

Jesus, like the prophet Micah before him, believed God wants justice, and to charge any worshipper inflated prices, was unjust.

> "… the Lord has told you what is
> good, and this is what he requires
> of you: to do what is just ……"
> Micah 6:8(NLT)

What appears to have irritated Jesus to the point of action, was that the unjust monopoly system, was being practised in the Temple;

God's house.

What does Jesus clearing the Temple say to us today?

Firstly, I don't think Jesus' actions, were something he decided to do, the previous night. He might have finally decided to clear the Temple the previous night, but the conviction that this practice had to be stopped, may well have been a move he had decided was necessary over twenty years before that.

At the age of twelve, Jesus spent a number of days in the Temple, discussing religion with the teachers of the law and he surprised them with his knowledge. Maybe, even by the age of twelve, Jesus had concluded that the Temple courtyards were being used to rip off worshippers and pilgrims to Jerusalem and it was a practice that should be stopped.

So is there any relevance of this example of Jesus clearing the Temple courtyard, for us today? At first glance there is no comparable activity in the Church today that Jesus would take a whip to.

How much focus on money is there, in the Christian Church today? Sometimes I suspect we have not analyzed what we are doing in the Church today, just as the temple rulers of Jesus time did not question the operation that they had going, within the outer Temple courtyard.

Perhaps the practices in the Temple courtyard, had become the norm over a long period of time. In other words, the practice that Jesus took a whip to, gradually crept in by a series of steps and as the practice became accepted, it was eventually justified.

There is another way to look at Jesus cleansing of the Temple. I have been raised in a middle class home, and the words of the Bible tell me to obey the recognized authorities. To quote the Apostle Paul.

> Everyone must submit to governing authorities. For all authority comes from God, and those in positions of authority have been place there by God….For authorities do not strike fear in people who are doing right, but in those who are doing wrong….Pay your taxes, too, for these same reason. For Government workers need to be paid.
>
> Rom 13:1-6 (abbrev) NLT

So my middle-class background, being raised in a loving Christian home, and the words of Paul, found a happy convergence. Placard-waving demonstrators, were the opposite of my psyche, upbringing, and faith.

Shortly after Paul wrote those words about obeying the authorities, he would be executed because of an illegal purge of Roman Christians by the Emperor, Nero. The execution of Paul and other Christians, would have been neither legal nor just, but the Emperor ordered it anyway.

So we Christians seem to have conflicting advice. To obey the laws of the land and yet there were instances in Jesus' life, the lives of the Apostles,   and the Old Testament prophets, where they disobeyed the laws and the authorities, when they believed laws were counter, to God's values.

Jesus, the prophets, and Apostles; recognised that sometimes a distinction had to be made between God's ways, and the rules of the authority in power.

In every age there are numerous secular laws to be obeyed, but also in every age there have been laws in conflict with God's values.

For example, to day, it is permissible in most countries to have repeat abortions, and in some countries,   abortions are even sanctioned.

There were two reasons Jesus ignored the rules or regulations of his time. When they prevented him from doing good (such as healing a man with a withered hand in a Synagogue on the Sabbath) and when he wanted to bring an end to dishonest and unjust practices, such as in,   the Temple courtyard.

With the picture of Jesus cleansing the temple, refusing to stop healing on the Sabbath or stop doing anything that he knew God wanted him to do, I wonder if that suggests that there are times when we as Christians need to be outside of our Churches, both individually and collectively, making a stand.

I am not going to suggest a particular cause or issue, as there are many, and one cause or issue may deeply concern some but not other Christians, to the same degree.

However, Jesus' example in the Temple asks the question. "When we become aware of an issue against God's purposes will you or I just stay within the comfort of our church and 'wring our hands' and say in despair, "the days are evil?" Or do we as individuals or groups, pick times and places where we will make a stand? It has been well said,

"all it takes for evil to flourish, is for good people to do nothing."

Take an example from the city, where I live. A rock station had pictures put up on some large bill boards, and those picture showed two men from their rear, with their pants down, walking towards animals. The pictures had been designed to shock people to read the ad, and they certainly did that.

 It did not take more than a second to recognize the depravity, this picture implied! The immediate question for me this large picture raised, was

> "Am I going to be a typical Christian and just wring may hands and say in despair. Our society is getting more and more evil by the day, and just let this billboard (and any that could potentially follow), stay there?"

The follow-up question was. "If this billboard is acceptable to our society, what other images will be permitted?" It seemed to me that it would be, open slather and while one or two images be a little lower; this one was not far, from the bottom.

My answer to the first question was.

> I am not going to be a typical, law-abiding, middle-class Christian. One who will meekly allow this type of picture to be displayed, without some kind of response. A response that says to the advertising agency, the rock station, the civil authorities and the rest of society - this type of picture is unacceptable to me,   both as a citizen and as a Christian.'

That answer raised a number of questions, each of which   held implications. Questions like.

- Is that type of advertising, acceptable to our law?

- If so, what can be done to change the law?

- If secular authorities will not change the law, what then?

Apart from the law, there were thoughts of a more immediate response. I toyed with possible responses. Do I and others stand there with placards reading something like, 'How low can we go?' Or perhaps I should drape a banner across the billboard with words, saying the same thing.

Follow up questions included. 'If I am to drape a banner across the billboard, should I do it at night, when no one will see me? Or during the day when it will be obvious? I thought of Jesus clearing the Temple during the day, and the answer was clear.

Jesus did it during the day, when he could be seen, and when he did it, he explained 'why' he was clearing the Temple. It is also implicit in Jesus' words before he cleared the Temple, that he knew there would be, unpleasant consequences.

When Jesus cleared the Temple, it was probably the last straw for the religious authorities, and after that they sought ways to arrest Jesus – legally or not.

As I contemplated what action to take, I began to think of possible consequences. It seemed shallow to think about consequences when I thought of some examples from the Bible and the consequences some Christians of our era, have faced.

Peter and John were whipped for preaching about Jesus. Shadrach, Meshach and Abednigo were thrown into a furnace and

Daniel a lion's den, because they would not worship a statue During WW 11, some Christians hid Jewish people to save them from the Nazis and any who were caught, paid dearly.

So as I thought about possible consequences to my actions, the worst of which may have been a fine – any consequences, were not worth mentioning   given the consequences Jesus, the Apostles,   prophets and some modern day Christians; have suffered.

 Of the immediate actions I considered at the time, the legal status of each, are outlined.

- Peaceful protest in front of billboard – legal

- Banner over billboard – possibly illegal?

- Defacing billboard – illegal and the least preferred option.

The sequel

The sequel to contemplating these various responses, was this. Before I took any of the above actions, another citizen looked at the city bylaws and discovered a law that said in effect.   It is illegal for billboards to show offensive images – and the billboards were removed.

That was the learning point, in this whole exercise, and should there be an issue in the future which I am not prepared to, 'just let things be', assessing the by-laws, is likely to be the first port of call.

Since then, I have thought of other possibilities. Calling talk-back radio. Writing a letter to the editor, of a local newspaper. Getting on Facebook or Twitter or some other online forum – and other possibilities.

In our world, there may be a justice or an injustice   issue, a Christian or group of Christians may feel compelled to act on. Or it could be a concern about the environment, or an ethical or moral issue. It could be that the Christian   faith   is   being   represented, prejudicially. For example, the way society is heading, it is becoming a crime to celebrate, Christmas.

There is no rule book stating,   what issue a Christian or group of Christians should take a stand on, or how.

In deciding to act or not to act, we have to consider Jesus and his actions, and the fact that each of us will have to give an account of our lives, to God. Rom 14:12

As I contemplated protesting against this billboard two 'balance' factors emerged. The first was the need for balance in my Christian life. To balance healing and reconciliation and standing up for what I believe, whether that is popular or not.

Jesus lived that balanced life. A life of faith and healing and forgiveness and love, while at the same time, opposing some of the unjust/ungodly practices of his time.

The second balancing act this billboard raised, was the need for a balanced message. To balance what I was *against,* with what I was *for*,

Jesus was *against* laws restricting him (or any person) healing or doing good to others on the Sabbath; and *'for'* - healing or doing good for others on the Sabbath.

Taking a stand. Because that billboard was in the open on main road, I was prepared to protest openly, even though I do not have a protesters gene, in my body. But maybe the word protest is the wrong word for some. Making a stand, is what any issue is about.

And it may be necessary to make a stand as a

Christian, in our families. In the wider family. In our schools or Colleges. In our community or club or organisation or place of employment.

In the bigger picture, secular society has been challenging and will continue to challenge the Christian faith, in three key areas. Our values, our beliefs and the credibility of our Holy Book, the Bible.

That billboard was an open way of saying. Your values do not matter. However, that billboard is just one part of a pervasive trend to display any image, apart from sex with under-age children.

At Discipleship books we believe all three are incredibly valuable, and there are excellent reasons to uphold, all three.

The way Jesus took a stand over some values of his time, contains a message for all Christians today.

I did not call you to follow me so that you will be comfortable. I called you to follow me so your ministry will be complete.

i.e. Have a complete ministry of healing and love and helping others, and taking a stand on important issues.

Chapter 6

What to take a stand on

Jesus analysed the religious system of his time. He listened to what the ordinary people were saying and how they justified their actions. Every time you read of Jesus saying, "you heard it was said.... That means he picked up a saying common at the time, but after reminding listeners of the common saying; introduced God's values

Jesus was aware of the power of the Romans and his philosophy was not to fight them, rather. "Render unto Caesar, that which is

Caesar's and to God, that which is God's. Jesus described the Jewish King who ruled in upper Galilee, a "fox."

Jesus was very astute in analysing what was going on the world of his time. He said, "the rulers of this age....

In our age, we need to make the same astute assessments that Jesus did. And it seems to me, that in western society, three key foundations of the Christian faith, are either ridiculed or ignored.

Christian moral values: Many in the secular world have made the mistake of assuming that the removal of moral constraints, equates to freedom. By contrast, the Christians view of moral laws is, they are like boundary posts - and living within those boundary posts, offers, true freedom.

Ignoring moral boundary posts, may 'seem' to offer freedom. In reality, ignoring moral boundary posts, leads to slavery. Money and glitz may 'seem' to offer freedom, but a secular reporter was honest enough to say, the people from a city like Las Vegas, seemed to be the "living dead". NZ Herald 11/5/2015

Obviously she was not describing all the people in the city or the Christians in that city, but that was her honest impression of the people she observed, in the street.

In our era, Christian morality is either attacked or ignored. What is promoted, is a philosophy of 'what is right for you is wrong for me and what is wrong for me, is right for you. Individual choice and individual morality is the key stone of Western thinking.

This self-centered philosophy ignores the crashes and heat-breaks that occur when people try to live life without any brakes. A British documentary titled 'Sun, sea and love cheats" which was about so called 'holiday romances' suggested they often lead to "heart break and financial ruin." Time Out Magazine 7-13 May

It is not often that secular programs are honest about the results of a self-centered individualistic morality, but it was refreshing that this documentary, was.

It was no different in Jesus' time. There were people like the Samaritan woman who was living with he 6th partner, who ignored moral boundaries. To the people of his time who jettisoned or scorned moral boundaries, Jesus made this comment.

"whoever sins is a slave to sin." John 8:34

In many movies today, there is the message that:

Cheating is liberating and violence and revenge, honourable actions.

With morality, we Christians need to be clear about what the key issue is - 'true freedom'. For most secular people, true freedom is the removal of moral constraints. For the disciple of Jesus, the core moral constraints, are the opposite. Boundary lines enclosing, true freedom.

Apart from the moral laws, there are Christian values like love, and justice and truth and mercy and grace and forgiveness. These values are worth, more than all the gold in Fort Knox.

Some in secular society recognise the worth of these values, but the implicit message of most advertising is. Success, ease, how we look, pleasure, security, popularity; are much more important.

The Christian Holy Book – the Bible.

In many institutions of higher learning they teach that the Bible contains, many mythological stories. It is hoped that sometime in the year 2016, this ministry will publish a book called   *Evidence the Bible is true,* detailing   reasons   to believe that every person and every significant event in the Bible, can be supported by archaeology and/or, internal evidence.

Christian beliefs.

Christians have a number of core beliefs, most of which are   captured in the creeds. Included among the beliefs questioned today, is whether there is a heaven or hell. The book, *Heaven is for Real,* is a wonderful answer to that question, but I have to point out. That book is only the latest in long series of books about those who have experienced heaven.

And books like that are tip of the ice berg, for many people have experienced the risen Jesus and heaven, but the majority of those experiences, have not been written down in a book.

For example, I have spoken with a very down to Earth person from a liberal denomination (that does not teach that heaven is for real), who told me about the time she was clinically dead (her heart was no longer pumping) and in that time she told me how she had met

Jesus, in a glorious place.

In Jesus time there were people called Sadducees who did not believe there was a heaven, and Jesus commented on their unbelief. "You do not know the Scriptures or the power of God." Matt 22:29.

The Christian belief that God created life is another area that secular society has, and will continue to challenge Christians over. By early 2016, it is hoped a book called "*Creation or Evolution. One of the two is unbelievable*", will be published.

The underlying theme of that book is, 'no thinking or informed person, could possibly believe life evolved by chance. By looking at all the evidence that is available, there had to be an incredibly intelligent, unseen creator responsible for life on this Earth.

Take the DNA which is in every species of plant and animal. Each plant and animal species only exists because there is this design package called, DNA. The official explanation for the acronym DNA is deoxyribonucleic acid.

Given that DNA is the body map or design code for each species; it seems more appropriate to say that DNA is the acronym for either. *Deities nucleic arrangement* or *Designers nucleic arrangement.*

At present, in the Temple of science, they convey the idea that only creationists, conservatives and fundamentalists, still believe God created life.

A   line that Jesus, if he were here on Earth today, would have challenged. That means it is up to us, his disciples, to question, the secular status quo that life evolved.

This is an important issue for Christians because, the building called the Christian faith, rests on the foundation that God is our creator. Among the beliefs that rest on that foundation are, these statements.

This is God's world. All people in it, were created by God, and therefore are of inestimable, importance. God holds the history of the world in his cusp.

 Christian values, the Christian holy book – the Bible and Christian beliefs are questioned, and often ridiculed, in secular society.

But because truth is paramount for Christians, and noting that 'truth' was a word, regularly on Jesus' lips, it is important that we Christians stand up for the truth.

That means, Christian moral values, Christian beliefs and the Christian holy book; are all, relevant, credible and true.   And Christian values, beliefs and Holy Book -   are all worth living out each day, and believing in. And in the unlikely event that we had to choose between valuing and not valuing these, they are worth, dying for.

Chapter 7

Other Religious Groups in Israel

As he grew up and before he began his ministry, I am sure Jesus looked long and hard at other religious groups in his country, perhaps asking himself, "Should I join them?" The question being,

"When I begin my ministry, should I begin it as a Pharisee? Or as a Scribe? Or as a Priest? Or as a zealot? Or as an Essene? Or as a Herodian, or some other political or religious group?"

Jesus did not begin his ministry till he was over thirty years old, so he had plenty of time to evaluate the various religious groups in his country. When Jesus was only twelve years old, he stayed on in Jerusalem for several days to discuss religion with the teachers of the law and they were amazed at his knowledge.

That implies, even then, Jesus had been thinking deeply about how religion was practised in his country. By looking more closely at the other religious groups in Israel at the time of Jesus, we can see why Jesus chose not to join them, and ended up with the ministry, he did

From the type of ministry Jesus chose, we can get insights into what is important for us as Christians today.

The Essenes
The Essenes were a religious group that Jesus could have joined, but chose not to. The Essenes had a community down by the Dead sea. They looked after one another and believed that to truly serve a holy God, it was necessary to be 'separate' from, the Godless in society.

The Essenes obeyed the laws, even more

strictly   than most Pharisees. The leaders of the Essenes had originally been Pharisees but decided they wanted to practice an even purer form of their religion. Regulations about the Sabbath for example, were even stricter that those applied by the Pharisees.

There are several obvious reasons why Jesus did not join the Essenes. Jesus came to establish the kingdom of God, a kingdom without boundaries. The community of the Essenes, had enforced boundaries, and only those 'approved' were allowed in or out.

 Another obvious reason Jesus did not join the Essenes, is this. Jesus said,

> "For the Son of Man came to seek and to save what was lost". Luke 19:10 (N.I.V.)

> "For I have not come to call the righteous, but sinners". Matt 9:13 (N.I.V.)

It would have been obvious to Jesus that those who joined the strict Essene community were 'the righteous', and not the "lost" or 'sinners' - the people he had come to seek and save.

An accusation the Pharisees levelled at Jesus

was that he "mixed" with sinners. Jesus' model of ministry, was to be among the lost sinners, and not separate from them, like the Essenes or Pharisees. Or in a few words.

Jesus' model of ministry was, not to be a light in a light-house. His model of ministry was to be a 'light in the darkness', and he encouraged his followers, to do the same. Matt 5:14-16 I.e. To be like salt or light.

The Sadducees.
The Sadducees were members of the priestly caste who generally observed the law and made some accommodation with the ruling Romans. One of the Sadducees belief's was that there was no resurrection, and by implication, no heaven. This must have grated with Jesus who said "You belong to this world here below, but I come from above".... John 8:23 (G.N.)

Jesus was not going to join a group who denied the existence of heaven, the place Jesus came from. He even knew the number of rooms in heaven. John 14:2 In Jesus' assessment, they did not know the Scriptures or the power of God. Matt 22:29.

The Scribes

Scribes have been described as a mixture of lawyer and theologian. They spent many hours in study to obtain the title of scribe, and once they had met the qualification, they were entitled to be called 'Rabbai' or teacher.

The zealots

The zealots were a group who were passionate (zealous) about observing the law. They lived zealously! From the perspective of the zealots, although the Romans provided a stable system of government, the Roman legions with their banners, represented a pagan power, headed by a god-like person called Caesar. Their desire was for a country, solely devoted to God.

The Zealots were also strongly opposed any Jew, they considered to be a Roman lackey. People like tax-collectors. By collecting taxes for the Romans, Jewish tax collectors (lackeys), enabled Rome to keep troops in their country.

Because of their opposition to the occupying Roman forces, Zealots believed they were 'doing God a favor' by killing a lone Roman who had let down his guard down, and sometimes they killed Jews, who they considered Roman lackeys.

Ridding the country of these godless Romans, was one of their key aims. Jesus had a very different philosophy to the zealots. He said, "Those who live by the sword, die by the sword. " Matt 26:52

Jesus also differed to the zealots in other ways. He proposed an attitude change, one that was the opposite of what zealots proposed. Instead of killing a lone Roman soldier like the zealots preferred to do, he urged his followers. If you are required by a Roman soldier to carry his load one mile, to carry it, two miles.

Imagine the scene. A Roman soldier approaches a Jew on the road and tells him, "I want you to carry my pack for a mile." The Roman soldier would most likely be used to Jews, bitterly resenting that request, and complying, very sullenly.

This time however, the Roman soldier has struck a disciple of Jesus who, instead of glaring at the Roman soldier for each step of the mile – whistles and sings hymns as they walk along while carrying the Roman's pack.

Then, when the mile is up, and when the Jewish citizen would normally, hurriedly, return the   soldier's pack. Instead of that, this disciple of Jesus insists on carrying the Roman's soldiers pack for another mile, all the while, singing hymns!

This picture of the disciple of Jesus carrying the Romans pack for 2 miles with a great attitude, suggests that when the Roman soldier returned to his barracks, he would says to his fellow soldiers, something like this. "If you are going to ask a Jew carry your load a mile, make sure he or she is not a disciple of Jesus – unless you are prepared to listen to Psalms and hymns for not one, but two miles!"

 That contrast between the practices of the zealots and the teachings of Jesus, can be found in other teachings. He   taught his disciples to love their enemies, even Romans. Matt 5:44 He demonstrated that love, when a Roman Centurion sent a message to Jesus, requesting he pray for his sick servant. This Jesus was happy to do, and the servant was healed.

By urging his disciples to love their enemy, that did not mean Jesus condoned, everything

Rome did. Jesus taught his disciples to "give to Caesar what was Caesar's, and unto God, what was God's." Matt 22:21(N.I.V.)

It was almost certainly not an accident that Jesus called a zealot (Simon) and a tax collector (Matthew), to become his disciples. After that, I am sure Jesus started to work on, both their attitudes.

Their attitudes to one another. To the occupying powers (in Simon's case), and to money - in Matthew's case.

The Pharisees

The Pharisees were only a temporary phenomenon in Jewish religious life, although some see a parallel to orthodox Jews, today. The Pharisees emerged after the exile in Babylon and disappeared after the destruction of Jerusalem, in A.D 70.

As a group, they were determined that they and their countrymen would follow God's ways - so that the disaster of the exile (which occurred because the nation had abandoned God and his ways), would never occur again.

As such, they were a group of people with the right goals. For the Jewish people to worship

God exclusively and live by God's laws. To achieve that goal and to make the laws more applicable, they gradually added to the commandments found in Exodus, Numbers, Leviticus and Deuteronomy.

 They eventually added another 600 laws to those laws found in the first five books of the Old Testament (the Pentateuch), resulting in over, 1200 laws to obey.

They Pharisees have been called "religious gate-keepers", for that is what they were, in their own eyes. In their own eyes, they represented true religion, and only allowed into their group, those who were following their laws exactly, and excluded those who did not obey their laws.

Because they saw themselves as religious gate-keepers, when new versions of the faith appeared, it was their job to ascertain if it was consistent with, or different to,   the true path they taught.

 And if it was different, they endeavoured to correct the errors taught by new teacher or group. That is why we read in the Gospels the Pharisees and teachers of the law coming to question Jesus.

"Then some Pharisees and teachers of the

law came to Jesus from Jerusalem and asked. "Why do your disciples break the tradition of the elders?" Matt 15:1&2 (NIV)

Jesus could have joined the party of the Pharisees, like the Apostle Paul after him, because many of Jesus' aims and those of the Pharisees, were the same, i.e. To do the will of God.

Having taken a long hard look at the way the Pharisees practised their religion, Jesus could see that their culture, values and practises, were very different from what God wanted and often   throughout the Gospels, Jesus is depicted clashing with the Pharisees or telling his disciples,   about the short-falls in their practises and teachings.

Following is a summary of the deficiencies Jesus identified in the religion practised by the Pharisees and teachers of the law.

- Concerned with outward appearance. Luke 11:43

- The mass of laws had become a burden. Luke 11:46

- Concerned with irrelevant detail Luke 11:42

- Not conducive to spiritual growth John 3:5

- Some of the man-made traditions cancelled out core commandments such as, looking after your parents. Matt 15:1-6.

- Was low on justice and mercy. Matt 23:23

- They obeyed their laws strictly, yet felt free to plan evil against vulnerable people not protected by the law. E.g. widows

Jesus regarded many of the additional laws the Pharisees added, as "Precepts of man" or "rules taught by men." Matt 15:9 (N.I.V.& NLT)

A few examples of these precepts of man or man-made rules. "It was a sin to walk more than 200 yards on the Sabbath or pick grains of wheat on the Sabbath or heal people on the Sabbath." Jesus by contrast believed that the Sabbath was made for the benefit of men and women. Luke 6:9

Though most of the practises of the Pharisees are viewed in an unfavourable light in   this chapter, a little balance needs to be in place -

because it is easy to become, anti-Pharisee through reading the Gospels.

Jesus was not anti Pharisee as much as he was, anti their attitudes and some of their practices. Nor were all Pharisees, anti-Jesus. Jesus accepted the invitation of a Pharisee to dine at his house, and Nicodemus (a Pharisee), came to talk Jesus privately about true religion. John 3:3

  Further, the risen Jesus called a fanatical Pharisee called Saul of Tarsus, to be his principal instrument to establish the Church among the gentiles. Acts 9:1-20

Jesus' purpose in rejecting so many of their religious ways, was not so that he could be a thorn in their side, but because he wanted to mould the religion, into one that God really wanted. One that would benefit worshippers. Jesus promised a religion that would offer freedom (John 8:32) and life to the full. John10:10

Jesus also wanted the people of his time to picture God - as he really was, and not the image they had as a result of looking through   the window-pane of the religion practiced by the Pharisees, and other religious groups.

We can see in Jesus' words, his passion to represent God, as He truly was.

> "Anyone who has seen me, has seen the Father." John 14:9 (NLT)

And

> *"the Father is in me, and I am in the Father." John 10:38 (NLT)*

Through these verses and   other verses, Jesus was essentially saying to those listening.

What you hear me say – that is what God would say.

What you see me do – that is what God would do.

The attitudes I have – they are the same attitudes, God has.

Attitude,   was   one of the distinguishing features between of the new Covenant religion of Jesus, and law based Covenant, of the Pharisees.

The Contrasts

Pharisees: Legalistic religion

Jesus: Grace-laced, religion

Pharisees: Only truth

Jesus: Grace and truth

Pharisees: Concerned with minute details of the law. Luke 11:42

Jesus: Concerned with the bigger picture, including, justice and mercy. Matt 23:23

Pharisees: The law comprised of hundreds of 'do not's.

Jesus: Made the law into a series of 'do's'. E.g. Matt 5:3-11

Pharisees: An obedience-based religion.

Jesus: An attitude-based religion.

An attitude based religion in which people were encouraged to: love God, love other people and love oneself. In the attitude-based religion Jesus introduced, he encouraged his disciples to 'desire' righteousness and desire mercy and desire peace.

So instead of doing these things because they could be censured or expelled if they did not do them - Jesus changed the religion into one which the disciples would, love to and desire to, obey the core* of the law.   See Matt 5:3-11

Pharisees doubled the number of laws from 600 to 1200

*Jesus: *Reduced the 600 laws to a much more manageable two, while holding to the Ten.*

Pharisees: Judged and condemned those who sinned. Luke 18:11(N.I.V.)

Jesus: Did not condemn or judge people who sinned.

NB Jesus did not condemn or judge people, but neither did he condone sin. It is implied from his words that Jesus did not condemn or judge people, because he knew what they were trying to achieve by sinning. I.e. They were trying to achieve, life, happiness and freedom. In various   teachings,   Jesus promised   these same three commodities (life, happiness and freedom), to any person who became a follower of his.

Pharisees: Defined doing good to others.

It was measured, and to whom was specified. I.e.   Certain   groups   were   excluded. Sometimes they avoided doing good to others by declaring something they possessed (and which could have been given to someone in need), "corban" - meaning, dedicated to God.

So, even though they had something to give to people in need, and it may have been their parents or children, they held onto it by declaring, it was God's or "corban".

Jesus: Offered no definitions of how or to whom and how much good, could be done to any person. Instead he taught a principle,

"Do unto others as you would have them do to you." Math 7:12.

That is a principle that can   be applied to: any person, anywhere, anytime,   by any means and by any measure.

Pharisees: In the view of the Pharisees, God only loved Jews, and particularly, Jerusalem Jews. That is, Jerusalem Jews in preference to, Galilean Jews.

Jesus: Taught his disciples to love all people regardless of race, gender, socio-economic status or any other status.

Pharisees: Preferred to be seen doing religious activities such as fasting, giving and praying.

Jesus: Urged his disciples to do these same activities, but in private, so that only God would notice.

Pharisees: In the religion of the Pharisees, relationships appear to be of, little value.

Jesus: Had a close relationship with his disciples, with the Holy Spirit and with his Father in heaven.

Pharisees: The concept of being born of the Spirit, was unknown.

Jesus: Considered it essential to be born of the Spirit so that they would, not only know the law, but the God who gave it. John 3:5

Pharisees: By obeying the many laws and rituals, there was no need to rely on the Holy Spirit.

Jesus: His ministry was,   Holy Spirit-dependent.

Pharisees: In the ritual-based religion of the Pharisees, there was little need for faith

Jesus: In the religion of Jesus, faith was the key to opening God's hand, because Jesus knew, the nature of God's heart.

Pharisees: Salvation through the blood of lambs.

Jesus: Salvation through the blood of The lamb.

Pharisees: Worship can only take place in the Temple or a Synagogue.

Jesus: Worship can take place anywhere, including the Temple or a Synagogue.

Pharisees: Called sinful people "sinners"

Jesus: Called sinful people "lost"

Pharisees: Avoided sinful people.

Jesus: Sought them out. He talked, wined and dined with sinful people.

<u>To summarise.</u>

From the above examples, it is obvious that Jesus words, actions and attitudes differed;   across the board, from those of the Pharisees. If Jesus had tried to join them, he   would have been like a square peg, trying to fit into, a round hole.

From Jesus teachings, there is a clue that he had considered joining the party of the Pharisees, then rejected the idea - for of all of the above reasons. He said:

"And no one pours new wine into old wine skins. If he does, the wine will burst the skins, and both the wine and the wine-skins will be ruined. No he pours new wine into new wine-skins. Mark 2:22 NIV

These words suggest that Jesus considered joining the Pharisee movement, then rejected that idea, concluding. His new wine, would burst the old wine skins of Pharisaic religion and so   he required no wine-skins, filled with the wine of his new religion*.

*It was essentially a reshaping of the old religion. Keeping the best and discarding the unnecessary; and an introduction of new attitudes, while relying on the Holy Spirit.

Jesus recognised that his:

Simplified, freeing, healing, truth-focussed, grace-laced, people-valuing, faith-encouraging, mission-directed, kingdom-building, Holy Spirit-dependent religion based on attitudes, rather than the law - would burst the old wine skins.

That is why he set out to create new wine skins from the first disciples, filled with the new wine.

Thank God, Jesus succeeded in creating new wine-skins from the first disciples and we who follow, are the new wine-skins, with the privilege of living out his, new-wine religion.

Chapter 8

Prophet, Priest and King

Many people of Jesus' time, did not know what to call him. Some called him a prophet, and others a teacher. His disciples eventually called him the Messiah which means – the anointed One, but initially they were at a loss, what to call him.

If the people of his time were unsure of the most appropriate title to call Jesus, that was because Jesus ticked so many boxes and deserved to be called: Teacher, Messiah;

Prophet, Priest and King.

Jesus, the King

The words of a familiar carol are, "born a child and yet a king." Jesus wore the garb of an ordinary person of those times, yet there was something about him that suggested, he was also, a king.

Though outwardly he wore ordinary clothes, by his words and manner suggested he was a king.

A King, robed in truth and justice and his crown contained the sparkling jewels called – lover of God and lover of people. Around his waist was a sash, with the words printed on it in royal blue – FREEDOM.

Faith in the love and power of God, blazed from his royal orb – the one he used when he reached out, to touch people. And on his feet, were the dazzling shoes of the Gospel of peace.

The people of that time noted that he was king over demons, and king over nature, and king over sickness. He was the king of provision, the one who turned water into wine, and five loaves and two fish into a storehouse of food.

Then there was the way he spoke. Matthew

recorded that the crowds were amazed because he "taught as one who had authority" – the authority of king. Matt 7:29 NIV

Unlike the teachers of the law, who, when they wanted others to take notice of what they were saying, referred to the words of some other great teacher, to help buttress what they said. However, King Jesus never did that. There was a royal authority to his words.

The first line of many of his teachings were, "I tell you the truth..." There was no uncertainty about this king. No reference to what any other person said. This king, simply told the people the truth.

But there was a purpose to Jesus telling the truth all the time. That purpose was, to set people free and lead them to true life.

His words and manner defined Jesus as, king, but also the power of God. When Jesus calmed a storm, the disciples exclaimed - "even the winds and the waves obey him!

A Prophet

A prophet is someone who knows, both the heart of God, and the heart of people. For much of his ministry, Jesus was like a prophet, in tune with the heart of God and also, where his people were at.

As a prophet, Jesus was aware of how people justified their actions. For example, Jesus said. "To what can I compare this generation?" Matt 11:16 Jesus knew the thinking, of the people of his generation. Speaking about some of his generation, he said they are:

"... like children playing a game in the public square. They complain to their friends,

We played wedding songs,
and you didn't dance,
so we played funeral songs,
And you didn't mourn."
Matt 11:17 NLT

What Jesus was meaning, is this. Some people in his time rejected his call to give up everything and follow him (even though he promised they would find life) because Jesus was too happy – like the happiness at a wedding. Others justified not becoming a disciple of Jesus because he was too serious - like words spoken at a funeral.

That analysis by Jesus (the prophet), has a contemporary ring to it. If Christians today are happy, people who have no wish to become disciples of Jesus, say. "Oh, they (Christians) are just a happy/clappy crowd." However if Christians warn them that they will ultimately give an account of their lives to God, they say. "You Christians are prophets of doom."

Can you see what Jesus was getting at? People will justify their decision,   not to become one of his disciples; either because we are too happy or, too serious.

Jesus as prophet, also addressed the relativist thinking in the people of his generation. The people of his time who said, "what is right for you is wrong for me with the comment, "whoever sins, is a slave to sin."

Jesus, being a prophet, was also aware of the things that people of his time, worried about. He recognised that many worried about: how they looked or where their next meal was coming from, or about the future. So Jesus addressed their concerns, in his teachings.

He asked those listening to him, why they worried about having enough food, as if God could not, and would not, provide. Matt 6:25-27

And to those worried about whether their clothing was fine enough, he made a comparison to the beautiful flowers of the field who God clothes in magnificent finery. Matt 6:28-31

And to those worried about the future, he said in as many words. Just be concerned about today, and God will take care of tomorrow. Matt 6:34

Jesus, the prophet, understood the ordinary people of his time, and felt compassion for them.   The   majority were in his view, "harassed and helpless, like sheep without a shepherd." Matt 9:36

Jesus the prophet, recognised that they were harassed by the religious authorities, who wanted the people to obey over a thousand laws, concerned with petty detail. But it wasn't just the religious authorities with their many demands, that harassed the people of his time. They had many other options to choose from, each of which may have seemed to offer, some direction or purpose in life.

They had the option of being wowed by

Roman power, or wowed by Greek culture. Or becoming a Herodian (supporter of King Herod), or joining one of the many religious groups,   detailed in the chapter 'Other religious groups in Israel'.

Or throwing in the religious towel altogether, like the Samaritan woman Jesus met at the well. A woman living with a man after having had, five previous husbands.

So what were the people to choose? The Roman way, the Greek way or follow devious Herod? Should they become a zealot or a Pharisee or Sadducee? Or become a person who adopts, some religious practices without becoming too serious about   religion. Or, throw the whole lot, overboard?

In Jesus view, the majority were, like sheep without a shepherd. That is how a true prophet thinks. They take a whole-nation' view, asking questions like. How are they doing? Where are they going and are they on track, to find real life?

On another occasion, Jesus revealed that he had the heart of a prophet, That was the time Jesus was speaking to the crowds and he exclaimed.

"O Jerusalem, Jerusalem, you who kill the prophets and stone those sent to you, how often I have longed to gather your children together, as a hen gathers her chicks under her wings, ... Matt 23:37 NIV

Prophets are often pictured as people who stand on street corners, fearlessly proclaiming God's judgement on people, and warning them to change their ways.

That was true of Jesus, he spoke of ultimate judgement, though he did not stand on street corners when he spoke about judgement. He did it through telling stories, which we call, parables and by getting listeners to ask questions   about   their   own,   life-style. Questions like.

"What does it profit you if you gain the whole world, but lose your soul?"

There are other sides to prophets, apart from the way they warn people of eventual judgement. True prophets, are people with, broken hearts! They recognise like Jesus that many are "harassed and helpless or lost, and

they grieve over their helplessness or lostness.
True prophets grieve, like Jesus did, over the people of Jerusalem, who; instead of welcoming God's prophets with banquets and allowing them to speak God's message, stoned them.

Another side to the nature of prophets, is that prophets desire that people find 'life' and 'happiness' and 'freedom' The goal of true prophets is that they try to direct listeners in the direction of, life, happiness and freedom.

Judgement is the ultimate end of a self-centered, God-rejecting life but what motivates true prophets, is a desire for people to choose the pathway that is the opposite of that pathway. To choose life, instead of death. For them to have eternal life with God instead of eternal separation, from God.

The desire that people choose life, is evident in the words of the prophet as Isaiah. He said (pleaded)

Come, all you who are thirsty...
Listen, listen to me, and eat what is good,
and your soul will delight in the richest fare.

Isa 55:1&2 NIV

Isaiah's heart and Jesus' heart, were the same. That God's people find the best and forget the rest.

Prophets recognise that lost people, are lost, are usually seeking three things. Happiness, freedom, and   life, and it is no coincidence that they   are the three things which Jesus offered his followers. Matt 5:3-11,   John 8:32 & John 10:10

As a prophet, Jesus not only analysed what people thought. I.e. Their worries and fears, what they were doing to God's message and messengers. Their attempts to find freedom and life, he also assessed the nature of the power brokers, or giants in the land. The giants who influenced the lives, of the lost sheep.

   There were three obvious power brokers (giants) in the land of Israel, during his time on Earth.

The religious authorities

The religious authorities who had significant wealth* and power, including powers to detain and arrest people. * Approximately 13% of a person's income, was paid in religious taxes. Jesus comprehensive assessment of the religious of the time, has already been detailed in chapter 5. Most of his assessment was not complimentary as were the reasons he rejected their wine.

King Herod

Another power broker (giant in the land) was King Herod. Along with the religious authorities and the Romans, he had the power to arrest people. He had John the Baptist arrested and later executed. He would execute anyone, not in favour of his rule.

To support his cause, there was a party called the Herodians.

Jesus called King Herod, a "fox". Luke 13:32 That was Jesus' assessment of him. A fox is an animal that prefers to sneak in at night and take unguarded chickens. Need we say more about Jesus assessment of King Herod.

The Romans.

Jesus could have urged his followers fight the Romans with hit and run tactics, like the zealots. Or to eventually fight the Romans in a conventional war. One he predicted would come, and which began in AD 66.

However, Jesus chose a different way to conquer the Romans - by conquering their hearts. He did this by teaching his disciples to love their enemies and, even go the extra mile for them. When questioned about whether it was appropriate to pay taxes to either to Rome or God. Jesus answered, both. Matt 22:21

- - - - - - -

You may be saying, OK Jesus analysed the power brokers of his time, but there are no powerful kings in our era, or religious authorities who collect taxes and have powers of arrest; or occupying forces such as the Romans.

 While that may be literally true, figuratively there are occupying powers or giants in every country, and as followers of Jesus, we need to ask at least three questions

- Who are they?

- How do they impact our lives as both citizens and Christians - and the nation as a whole?

- What influence do I accept and reject?

I suggest the power brokers in our time are:

- Governments. Federal and State

- Educational institutions

- The Advertising industry

- The media.

- The film industry

A full analysis of the effects of these giants, is a separate book, but we need to be aware of both the good they are doing for our country, and the harm, just like Jesus was in his time.

Take the results of a survey of what teenagers worry about and this analysis comes from a book called, *The Teenage Brain.*

This book identified the five most frequent worries of teenagers and also the five most intense worries of teenagers. The most intense worries of the teenagers surveyed, were in order of intensity. (1) War (2) Personal harm (3) Disasters (4) School (5) Family.

No 1, greatly surprised me. Why are teenagers worried about war, 25 years after the end of the cold war? If that survey was conducted during the cold war era, I could understand teenagers being worried about war and possibility of nuclear annihilation. That was a very real possibility during the cold-war era, but why are teenagers today, in the post cold-war era,   worrying about war?

My answer is this, and my take does not result from any research, rather it is gut-feeling response, to what I see. So many computer games, are war games, of various kinds. Our news bulletins, are dominated by reports of wars and conflicts and violence. Movies and T.V programs dominated by conflicts. Movies about the goodies combating evil, alien empires or rogue states, or wars begun by rogue geniuses with some deadly new weapon, intent on destroying the human race.

At the time of writing, most new movie releases seem to be about war against some ugly foe; and this foe is combated by a person Mr good-guy, holding lethal guns. So is it any wonder, teenagers have a deep seated fear, or war?

The follow up question,   is obvious. How much are we Christians going to allow ourselves,   and our families,   to be bombarded with this pre-occupation with war by war gamers, the news media, and the movie moguls?

Jesus began his teaching ministry addressing some of the fears or worries of the people of his time, and I suggest those worries have changed little, with the passage of time.

Another power broker in our time, is the advertising industry and here I am not picking on any individual advert, but the overall effect of most ads.

 There is an underlying message in many ads that you and I will be much happier, 'if' we buy a certain product!' The smile on the face of the person selling the product, tells you they have at last found happiness, when they began using the product being advertised.

Rubbish! Life may be a little easier if you or I buy a certain product, but then again. It may be no easier than if we bought, another companies products. Ultimately and more importantly; no product can give us, happiness.

Giving and blessing others, will bring us true happiness. Serving God, is a pathway to, true happiness. Experiencing the joy of the Holy Spirit, is a factor in true happiness, because that joy is not dependent on circumstances.

There is also an implicit message to 'some' adverts, which is. "You and I will be more important and valuable, if we buy, certain products."

I hope Christians do not buy into that, implicit message. Rather they will say. "I am a child of God, and nothing I buy or don't buy can add or subtract, from my eternal value."

What has this to do with Jesus. A lot actually. He urged his disciples and those listening to question where their happiness came from and the gods in their life. He did so by asking questions like. "What will it profit you... or "Why do you worry about...

Enough about the giant, called the advertising industry and I need to add. I am not anti-the advertising industry and have in the past and will continue to advertise products in whatever medium seems best suited to the product being sold.

It is only over the issue of happiness and value; that we disciples of Jesus need to be wise enough to say. True happiness comes from owning possessions and neither does my value, as a person.

Other powers in the land include, State and Federal Governments. They determine how much is spent on the police, the environment, health, education. Government policies, dictate to a large extent, a country's values.

These sheep without a shepherd, may believe that a relationship with another person, will be, heaven on Earth! Or making lots of money, will be, heaven on Earth. Or that taking recreational drugs will mean, heaven on Earth.

Schools, Colleges and Universities, are also significant powers in the land, influencing the thinking of yesterday's, today's and tomorrow's students. Most teach that life evolved rather than was created. In most the implicit attitude is, what you do in your private life is none of our business, so any sexual relationship over the age of consent, is OK.

The mind sciences (various schools of analysis) seem to offer wonderful new insights to help people, compared to say, relationship with Jesus. Asking him to come into our life, to change it for the better.

Yet a former psychologist did a survey of people counselled by counsellors of the various mind sciences, and admitted that those who had no counselling, were often more successful in working out a solution to their problems,   than those who received counselling from one of the   schools of analysis.

I don't wish to knock trained therapists, but for a number of reasons I have gone beyond being wowed by the insights of various schools of analysis, and concluded that the main beneficiaries of mind sciences, are. The people who are already psychologically healthy, and those who do the analysis.

Questioning secular solutions to life's problems is what Jesus did, and what we, his disciples, need to do. Apart from that, Jesus analysed the philosophies and gods, the people of his time had.

In our day there are many philosophies and gods which people live by, and worship. These philosophies are substitutes for the teachings of Jesus and the gods, substitutes for the real God.

Those   substitutes,   may   include: the environment becoming god, outdoor activities, wealth creation, success, sports, a sports team, meditative practices, a philosophy, addictive substances, sex, a political party or .... and other

It is often implied in Colleges and Universities

that committed Christians are unthinking and unquestioning people. Rather, the opposite is true. The true disciple of Jesus is a thinking/questioning person who will question everything including; secular models, beliefs and trends.

The trend in modern society towards; me-ism, consumerism, philosophy, the mind sciences, humanism and relativism*.

*Hitler was a relativist. He determined his own values by his own standards and thinking.

Jesus, being a prophet, questioned the beliefs, value systems and schools of thought of his time, so when we question some of today's trends and values, we are being; true followers of Jesus.

In his day, Jesus, being a prophet, had a heart for those seeking life and happiness in false gods and legalistic religion. His prophet's heart cried out, "O Jerusalem, Jerusalem...."

He would like us to have the same heart. Not one that cries, not "O Jerusalem, Jerusalem"... like Jesus did. But a heart that cries

"O America.." or "O Britain... or "O Australia...

or "O Canada.. or "O Singapore ..or "O China or "O South Africa... or "O ....

Fill in the name of your country, if not mentioned.

That like Jesus, we recognise that many people of our time are also like, sheep without a shepherd. They are not sure, where to turn to, for salvation.

Whether to turn to health foods for salvation, or Buddhism or Islam. To make technology or the social media, their god? Or whether to make their Messiah; a military hero or a sports coach or an author or an activist or a political leader or a scientist?

There are many pathways that seem to lead to salvation but Jesus will always be, "..the way, the truth and the life. ". John 14:6

The Priest

The writer of the book of Hebrews explained to readers how Jesus was/is, both the sacrifice necessary to wash away sins, and the Great High Priest spreads the blood on the altar, as a sacrifice. See Hebrews chapter 8.

Jesus laid the foundation for that post-resurrection theology by telling listeners. "I am the way, the truth, and the life. No one comes to the Father except through me." John 14:6 NIV

 A Priest, and particularly the High Priest, represents God to people, and people to God, and I suggest that people of Jesus' time saw in his words, his actions and the miracles he did; God

Jesus was not like a priest, serving in the Temple, but many perceived him to be a Priest. He talked with confidence about God. Some of his teachings were in essence. God is like this....Not may-be or possibly.

In a number of teachings, Jesus made it clear to those listening, that though he was speaking, it was as if, God was speaking. Jesus said to Philip. "anyone who has seen me, has seen the Father." John 14:9 NIV

A number of religious teacher were like that. Outwardly, Jesus was just a carpenter from Nazareth who had embarked on a teaching ministry, but.... something about his manner.

Something about the certainty with which he taught and from the various reports. Walking on water, healing the sick. Rebuking storms, raising the dead – there were too many signs saying, this man is, close to God. Closer than even the High Priest.

So a man, though schooled in the religious teachings of his time, came up to Jesus and, being desperate to get in touch with God, asked, "Teacher, what good can I do to inherit eternal life?" Matt 19:16 NIV

This religious teacher had not found in his extensive religious training, an assurance that he was going to inherit eternal life but something about who Jesus told him that Jesus - the High Priest, would be able to provide, that answer.

Jesus was like a Priest to many at that time. Bringing people to God and God to people. Even on the cross, Jesus was like that. He said to a condemned criminal whose life was ebbing away, "today you will be in paradise with me." Luke 23:43

That is a role of Christian leaders, but also each Christian, imperfect though we are. We can be like a Priest, to the people we meet during the course of our daily lives.

Helping people get in touch with God, and God with people because we know how much; God would love to be their God and have a relationship with them.

What the disciples did

Chapter 9

The disciples respond

The first disciples, obviously did not know the key theme of this book because they lived about two thousand years before it was written, but both during Jesus' ministry and after the coming of the Holy Spirit in power, began to live as servants or ministers of the Gospel.

A hymn written several hundred years ago, captures the essence of servant discipleship. It is a hymn I call, "the disciples hymn."

Take my life, and let it be
consecrated, Lord , to Thee.
Take my moments and my days;
Let them flow in ceaseless praise.

Take my hands, and let them move
At the impulse of Thy love.
Take my feet, and let them be
Swift and beautiful for Thee.

Take my voice, and let me sing
Always only for my King
Take my lips and let them be
Filled with messages from Thee

Take my silver and my gold;
Not a mite would I withhold.
Take my intellect and use
Every power as Thou shalt choose.

Take my will, and make it Thine
It shall be no longer mine.
Take my heart - it is thy own;
It shall be Thy royal throne.

Take my love; my Lord I pour
At thy feet its treasure-store
Take my self, and I will be
Ever, only, all for thee!
Frances Ridley Havergal, M.H.B
400

Following on are examples of ways, the first

disciples began to live their servant discipleship.

Take my love, my Lord I pour.
When a woman who had lived a sinful life in that town, learned that Jesus was eating in the Pharisee's house, she brought an alabaster jar of perfume, and as she stood behind him at his feet weeping, she began to wet his feet with her tears. Then she wiped them with her hair, kissed them and poured perfume on them. Luke 7:37-38 (N.I.V.)

Take my intellect and use, every power as Thou shalt choose.
Jesus called Matthew to be a disciple. Matthew's job had been as a tax collector. A job that required Matthew to   record meticulously, the details of each citizens assets, income and consequently the amount of tax they were required to pay. About thirty years after Jesus ascended to heaven, Matthew eventually used his familiarity with detail and information, to write the Gospel of Matthew.

Take my lips and let them be, Filled with messages from Thee.
Day after day in the Temple courts and from house to house, they (the disciples) never stopped teaching and proclaiming the good

news that Jesus is the Christ. Acts 5:42 (N.I.V.)

Take my silver and my gold, not a mite would I withhold

Zacchaeus said "Look, Lord! Here and now I give half of my possession to the poor, and if I have cheated anybody out of anything, I will pay back four times the amount". Luke 19: 8(N.I.V.)

Mary, Joanna, Susanna and other women helped support Jesus and the twelve, out of their own purses. Luke 8 :1-3

Joseph of Aramathea laid Jesus' body in a family tomb hewn out of rock. Because these tombs were hewn out of rock by hand, only the wealthy could afford to have one made- and it is likely that Joseph had this tomb hewn out so that family members could be laid there, when they died. After Jesus' death, Joseph made the family tomb available for Jesus' body. Matt 27. 57-60

Take my voice and let me sing, always only for my King.

> "..the whole crowd of disciples began joyfully to praise God in loud voices for all the miracles they had seen;   Blessed is the king who

comes in the name of the Lord! Peace in heaven and glory in the highest." Luke 19: 37-38 (N.I.V.)

Jesus pictured discipleship as being like an easy fitting and gentle yoke. He also pictured his disciples as being like salt and light. We are like salt and light, when we offer him our hands, our love, our intellect, our money, and our words, for his service.

When each Christian is doing that, individually they become like a light, but collectively like a chandelier, emitting blazing light.

Chapter 10

My utmost for his highest

Several decades ago I noticed a sign on the wall of a Church hall. That sign may have already been there for 30-40 years - looking at the state of the varnish on the wood. The words on the sign read,

My utmost for his highest.

Those words seem to capture the nature of our call, to be disciples of Jesus. He comes into our life to be, Lord of all. He calls us to make the kingdom of God, our first priority. He calls us to, deny ourselves, and take up our cross, and follow him. He calls us to give up everything, for the sake of the Gospel and follow him.

So those few words, 'My utmost for his highest', seem to capture all those thoughts about the cost and the priority discipleship in our lives – for the sake of King Jesus.

Sometimes however, that call to give 'our utmost for his highest', can be, if we are not wise, a cocktail for burnout. That is, unless we are being honest with ourselves about what we are trying to achieve and why we are trying to achieve it; and how.

Subconsciously, a Christian might try to be *all things to all people*, and try to do *everything.* These are typical factors in, discipleship burn-out.

Along with our commitment to give our, all for his highest, we Christians need to be wise enough and honest enough to acknowledge our limitations. And somewhere along the discipleship journey, we need to learn to distinguish between what is important, and what is necessary. Between what is good and what is godly.

At the time of writing these paragraphs, i decided to withdraw from a management position that required a lot of decision making. A position that was good for me, because it utilised my decision-making   abilities and others in the firm; both those under me, and those above, appreciated my work - but.

At the same time I was in this management position, I was also trying to finish 6 books in my spare time and trying to spend time with my wife and family and spend time with friends,   and at Church and have time for recreation and, and .....

 Soon I began to run out of steam and found it hard to concentrate. I became   irritable and tired and began to snap at those close to me. It soon became obvious that I had allowed myself   to   become   over-loaded   with commitments and was trying to do too much - to the detriment of virtually everyone and everything in my life.

It was obvious, it was time to take   the scissors to some part of my busy life, and to cut back, somewhere.

Time with my wife and family and friends and Church, were non-negotiable. The desire to finish the books the Holy Spirit had prompted me to write, was also, non-negotiable. The only other possible way of   restoring   my energy, was to withdraw from that management position, and take a lesser position in the company.

After that, I was able to recharge my batteries for what was ultimately, more important. The choice was between, the good and the godly. Between what was important and what was, ultimately important.

Jesus calls us to partner with him in building the kingdom. However, in that partnership, he will not make us or force us to:

- Exercise wisdom.

- Exercise self control about how many activities we are involved in.

- Identify what are our gifts, and what are not

- Identify what is on our heart so we can focus on those heart-tasks, to exclusion of many other worthy tasks, in the kingdom

- Allocate time for important people in our lives

- Allocate time to recharge our batteries each week.

- Make us take a vacation – and the occasional sabbatical leave.

All of these, Jesus leaves up to us.

In the example cited, I chose to cut back on commitments to secular work so that I would have time to focus on writing books (my heart-task), family, friends, church and recharging my battery.

Earlier in life I chose to withdraw from small group leadership in our Church, something I was just 'cut out to do', in order to concentrate on a health issue in my home, and my secular work.

With that earlier example, it was my commitments at Church, that were put aside, in favour of work and family. In the latter example, it was the secular work commitments that were lessened, in favour of my family and Christian commitments.

The key verse in this part of the chapter, is,

Jesus was in the stern, sleeping....Mark 4:38

Jesus did not try to do everything. He did not try to save the world, rather, he urged the disciples to do that. He did not even try to save the Roman Empire. Jesus could have gone to Rome or Athens to speak, obvious stepping stones to save the Roman Empire.

 Instead of that, he largely confined himself to a very small area of the Empire - and then it was only for a three year period. The extent of Jesus' ministry trips covered an area of no more than, 100 miles by 30 miles

At times Jesus is pictured, sleeping in boats, picking corn, wining and dining (something his enemies criticised him for) and he must have stopped to notice how the beautiful lilies were, because he commented on their beauty. Matt 6:28

Sometimes, Jesus spent time alone. On another occasion he took three disciples with him for an over-nighter, on a mountain. Other times he was alone with the twelve. Other times he was in a family home which Mark simply refers to as "the house".

Western Christians are often terrific at doing but not so good at just being - or praying or meditating. It is possible to be 'nicer than Jesus' and avoid ruffling feathers (like Jesus did in   the Temple) and it is possible to be, 'busier than Jesus'.

When we run out of steam or our health breaks down, it is usually not hard to analyse the reasons why. Ego has perhaps, quietly hitched a ride, as if to say. "You can do anything and everything. You have both natural and spiritual gifts and skills, which are 'needed' by the Church!"

Subconsciously we can be thinking. I am indispensable and irreplaceable – and our body gets over-taxed, as a result.

While we will undoubtedly have natural and spiritual gifts to offer, if ego has hitched a ride, we can get, over committed. Satan may have even get in on the act by playing a tune like that below. NB He sometimes quotes Scripture and is capable of summarising Scripture.

"Christians are meant to be a servants, and servants serve. The more you serve, the more-Christ-like you are."

While those words are an accurate description of the Christian life and   Jesus' style of leadership,   we need both wisdom and self control, as well. What greatly pleased God about Solomon at the beginning of his reign was, he asked for wisdom.

We need the wisdom to assess:

What can I achieve in the time available?

What is/are my heart motivations?

There are a thousand different ways to serve the Lord and he puts those thousand different passions on the hearts of,   thousands of different Christians, to meet the needs of the kingdom.   But the key question is. *What passion/s has he placed, on my heart?*

By focussing on what Jesus has placed on our heart and then getting involved in what the Lord has placed on our heart. And then by adding a little wisdom and self control – we become the effective disciples, Jesus wants us to be.

One undervalued fruit of the Holy Spirit is "self control". To the passion to serve Jesus (and give our utmost for his highest), wisdom and self-control are two great assets to carry with us, on our discipleship journey.

So on this journey of discipleship, why not,

(1) Do your best, and leave God the rest!

In this walk of faith, God can take care of anything we do not achieve today or this week or this month!

On that journey of discipleship, why not,

(2) Do your best, then have a rest!

In this walk of faith, we do not get fired, if we

get tired.

On this journey of discipleship, why not,

(3) Do your best, and make time for the rest!

I.e. There are other important people in our life   (who need our time). Special occasions to celebrate. Other tasks to achieve that also require time, and we need time to recharge our batteries.

NB Jesus was and is, the ultimate time-manager! He urged his followers to live for today and not to worry about tomorrow, while God is the ultimate, life-manager. He has plans for our lives, and those plans may include seasons, on the side-line. See Eccl 3:1

Appendix

So many of Jesus teachings and a number of the parables, were told to challenge the first disciples about the cost of discipleship and the kingdom was to have in their lives.

One of the main purposes of Jesus' ministry was to create a group of disciples who would become the core of the new Church, and then when he thought they were ready, he gave them what we call, the great commission.

In that commission, Jesus urged the first disciples, to go and make disciples of all nations ... Matt 28:19

There are two different aspects to the word disciple. The Hebrew and Greek rendering of the same word,   highlight two different aspects of discipleship.

The Greek word for a disciple is '*mathetes*'. The verb being *manthanein*, which means to learn by experience or practice. That suggests any disciple of Jesus had to 'learn' to become a disciple of Jesus by putting into practice, his teachings. I.e. It does not automatically follow that once a person has made a decision to follow Jesus and become one of his disciples, they will automatically put into practise all of his teachings.

 Every disciple has to 'learn' to be a disciple by putting into practice his teachings.

The other aspect of discipleship is emphasized by the Hebrew word 'talmid' from the word 'lamad', to learn. Knowledge of Jesus' teachings are gained by learning the teachings. Jesus said:

> "teaching them (that is, the new disciples from every nation) to obey everything I have commanded you." Matt 28:19 (N.I.V.)

Everything Jesus commanded? One Bible commentary identifies over three hundred different subjects that Jesus taught.

Discipleship is a learning process, and not a one- off event, and from my experience, one where we never fully arrive. When Jesus was with the twelve disciples, he described the process of discipleship like this.

> "Take my yoke upon you and learn from me, for I am gentle and humble in heart, and you will find rest for your souls. For my yoke is easy and my burden light." Matt 11:29-30 (N.I.V.)

A yoke is a wooden harness that is made to fit neatly and comfortably over the shoulders of an ox, and attached to a plow. The plow turns the earth over so that seeds can be planted. In today's terms we would say, the yoke was ergonomically designed. i.e. Designed to fit the body of the ox in the same way modern seats are designed to fit our body contours.

Jesus has a yoke of discipleship to put on our shoulders. It fits neatly and comfortably. That yoke of discipleship is designed to help us use our time, our abilities, our money, our possessions, and follow our heart passions - for the sake of the Kingdom of God.

In the book called *The Son,* the final pages were devoted to illustrating how Jesus, walked his talk. The word integrity comes to mind. Even his enemies admitted that much.

The concluding paragraph of that chapter, is worth repeating.

"I am proud to be a disciple of Jesus, because of what he said. I am proud to be a disciple of Jesus, because of what he did; but I am especially proud to be a disciple of Jesus because - both what he said and what he did, were one and the same!

Jesus was a servant king we can be proud to call, "Lord."